The Architect's Eye

E & FN SPON

An Imprint of Chapman & Hall

London · Weinheirn · New York · Tokyo · Melbourne · Madras

Tom Porter

The Architect's Eye

Visualization and depiction of space in architecture

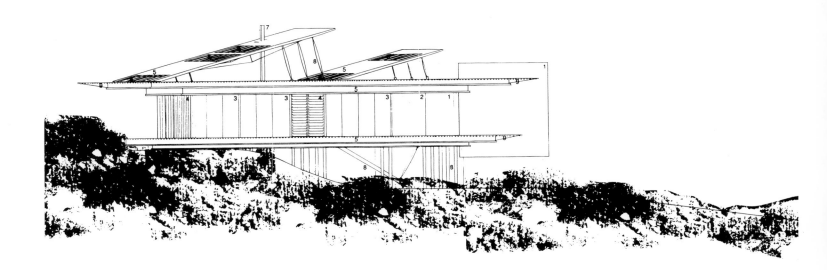

Published by E & FN Spon, an imprint of Chapman & Hall, 2-6 Boundary Row, London SE1 8HN, UK

Chapman & Hall, 2-6 Boundary Row, London SE1 8HN, UK
Chapman & Hall GmbH, Pappelallee 3, 69469 Weinheim, Germany
Chapman & Hall USA, 115 Fifth Avenue, New York, NY 10003, USA
Chapman & Hall Japan, ITP-Japan, Kyowa Building, 3F, 2-2-1 Hirakawacho, Chiyoda-ku, Tokyo 102, Japan
Chapman & Hall Australia, Thomas Nelson Australia, 102 Dodds Street, South Melbourne, Victoria 3205, Australia
Chapman & Hall India, R. Seshadri, 32 Second Main Road, CIT East, Madras 600 035, India

First edition 1997

Copyright © 1997, Tom Porter

Edited & designed by Conway Lloyd Morgan

Printed and bound in Hong Kong by Dah Hua Press Co.Ltd

ISBN 0 419 21230 2

Contents

**Title page illustration: Rendered
elevation for a villa in Corsica by
Jean Nouvel**

Acknowledgements

The author pays tribute to the memory of his friend and mentor, the late Jean Koefoed.

The author would like to thank the following for their generous support and help in supplying comment, encouragement and material during the course of this book's preparation:

James Allen, Phil Allison, Will Alsop, Fred Batterton, Giovanni Brino, Sue Brown, Marja van der Brugh, Richard Bryant, Anthony Caro, Costas Chronopoulos, Rebecca Davies, Ian Davis, George Dombek, Craig Downie, Kevin Forseth, Matt Gaskin, Ron Hess, NIgel Hiscock, Mike Jenks, Benti Lange, Mike Leech, Jean Philippe Lenclos, Hiroshi Naito, Mette L'orange, Iradj Parvaneh, Martin Pawley, Alison Pearce, Alan Phillips, Agni Pikioni, Richard Rose-Casemore, Paul Rudolph, Chris Simpson, Shin Takamatsu, William Taylor, Petite Werenskiold Skaugen, Ken Whiting and Giuliano Zampi.

He would also like to thank Sue Goodman who made some of the line drawings.

A special debt is due to Conway Lloyd Morgan who, sharing a fascination for architectural representation, gave unstinting help in the design and production of this book

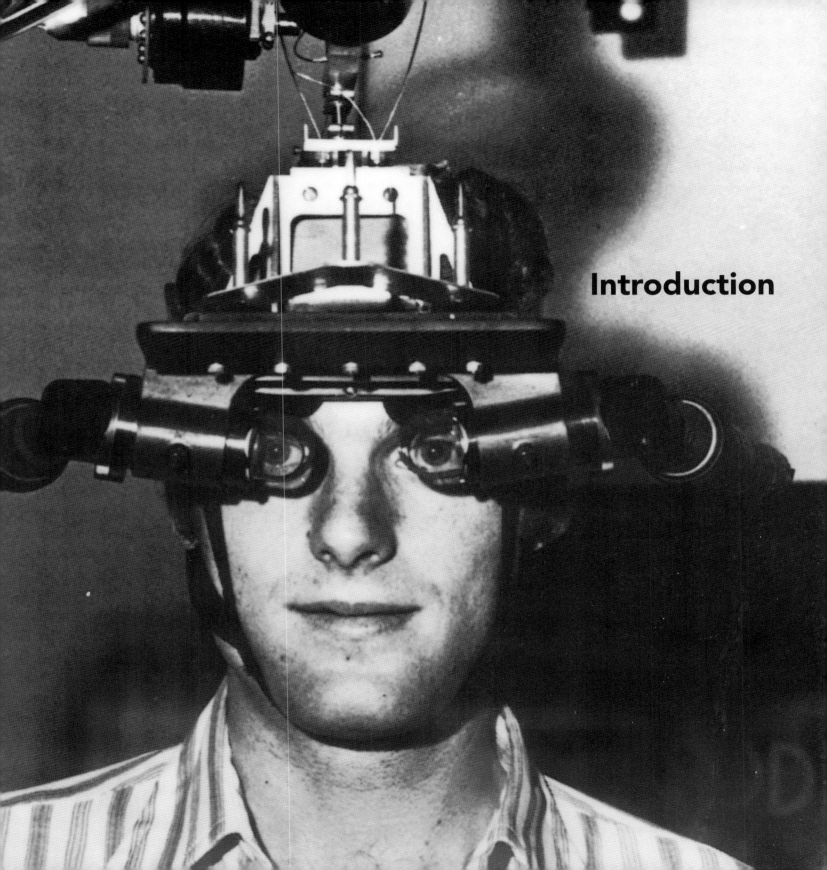

Introduction

Introduction

Although many books have been published that focus on architectural drawing, the immediate conversion of architectural ideas into two-dimensional 'models' has not always been central to the creation of the built environment. In more traditional structures - such as the Shinto temples in Japan and Nelson's flagship HMS Victory - construction was eyeballed, working directly into space entirely without the aid of any working or design drawings. The ancient Chinese builders of Ming and Manchu cities also worked without scaled drawings, relying instead on intricate small-scale models in plaster, which display a remarkable precision and elaboration.

The depth of spatial understanding in primitive and ancient cultures still perplexes modern science. For example, the meaning behind the Peruvian 'Lines' and the internal workings of complex labyrinths of space within some pyramids still remain unsolved despite the repeated probes of modern archaeology. The mystery surrounding the origins of such an ancient and profound command of space has triggered a plethora of speculation which ranges from the sensational idea of an extra-terrestrial instruction to the theory that prehistoric humankind was endowed with a sixth sense. The latter refers to the notion that our early predecessors could tune in to energy force-fields which enabled them to undertake extended journeys into the wild for food and flint. Set against this is the theory of ley lines first proposed by A. Watkins in 1925. He suggested that a landscape systematically littered with notched hillsides and strategically positioned stones shows that the primitive hunter moved with a full-scale 'map' of the environment. A remarkable grasp of an auditory plan of space is reflected in Professor Richard Carpenter's account of the Alaskan Aklavik tribe who can graphically record an accurate impression of the shape of islands at night by listening to the sound of waves lapping their shores.

Realizing that a first hand, conscious experience of space is important in the training of those who intend to articulate it, Leonardo da Vinci devised a series of games for his junior draftsmen. For example, in order to develop visual accuracy in judging dimensions, he proposed that a line be drawn on a wall and, standing approximately nine metres away, his students attempt to judge its length by cutting a straw - the one who cut his or her straw nearest the actual length won the game. A further diversion recommended by Leonardo involved judging depth by guessing the number of times the length of a thrown javelin was contained in the distance of the throw. Although Leonardo's games were intended to sharpen the visual skills of budding artists, it is even more critical for the environmental designer who employs a graphic design dialogue to engage in a direct experience of space.

This is, of course, because architecture is concerned with the physical articulation of space; the amount and shape of the void contained and generated by buildings being as material a part of its existence as the substance of its fabric. Other disciplines such as painting and sculpture are equally involved with spatial organization but in different terms. In that the role of the architect has gradually become more and more specialized, he or she has still to cope with the spatial variables of light, surface, shape and form although in almost complete isolation from the influence of other artists. As a consequence, the architect has adopted a private and mainly graphic language of design which can be more concerned with technique than with any experiential understanding of space.

We have only to consider the visual inadequacies of the modern environment or the findings of research programmes which examine its psychological effects to discover evidence that uninformed methods of representation can not only influence the formation of ideas but can predetermine the appearance of resulting architecture. It is against such a background that this book has been written, and in the awareness that design attitudes in education are often founded on the assumption that architecture is born within the confines of a flat, two-dimensional plane. Therefore, beyond an historical survey of the changing modes of spatial representation, its central aim is an understanding of the nature of space supported by a variety of physical and non-physical spatial concepts. Then follows a study of the elements governing spatial perception, a critical assessment of the perceptual viability of conventional design codes and, finally, a review of the alternative methods of externalizing spatial ideas - the latter including the enormous impact of the computer on the ability to enter the space of our imagination.

A Short History of Spatial Representation

'Space: that which is not looked at through a keyhole, not through an open door. Space does not exist for the eye only; it is not a picture: one wants to live in it.'

El Lissitzky

A Short History of Spatial Representation

The evolution of the link between architectural drawing and concepts of space in environmental design overtures can be traced back via a continuous, though threadbare, chain of evidence to the higher cultures of the Near and Far East and the Mesopotamian and early Egyptian dynasties when the idea of an architectural ground plan had already been developed and spatial concepts were organized against simple linear grids. The earliest drawings illustrate that such a system was already in use in Ancient Egypt where roughly scaled planes - elevations being much rarer - were drawn in black on small papyrus sheets squared in red pigment. Also, preparatory linear devices for the compositional arrangement of size and shape have been detected beneath Egyptian tomb painting. These were later dissected by the surgery of Constructivist and Neoplastic artists, such as Piet Mondrian and Theo Van Doesburg, who saw them as architectonic ends in themselves, and whose clear structures of geometric order had such a pruning effect on twentieth century architectural thinking.

Amongst the earliest known 'architectural' design drawings is a landscape layout plan for a tamarisk grove which fronted the Egyptian temple at El-Dier el-Bahari near Memphis (fig. 1). It is drawn in ink on a sandstone flake and dated *circa* 2100 BC. This particular drawing is remarkable as it shows how little the linear drafting of space has changed during the last 4,000 years. More interesting is Geoffrey Broadbent's speculation that the designer, possibly for the first time in the history of environmental design, made a crucial drafting error. His enthusiasm for the grid plan carried him away, for he extended the network into a neighbouring site; subsequent archaeological excavation revealed that his mistake was confined to the drawing as the actual grove was contained within the boundary of its original site. However, in attempting to penetrate the mysteries of the ancients' methods of visualization, some other studies suggest that it is unlikely that preparatory drawings were widely utilized in architectural design.

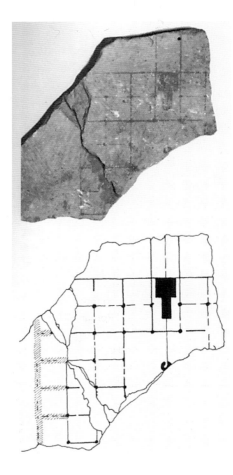

Fig. 1: The earliest evidence of an architectural drawing, and also of a planning mistake. Ink on limestone, 2100 BC.
Courtesy Metropolitan Museum of Modern Art, Museum Excavations, 1920-22, Rogers Fund, 1922.

If only half of the modern theorists are correct, the Great Pyramid, Stonehenge and other ancient monuments were built exclusively according to scientific needs. Their location, setting, size and shape were determined by the need to embody cosmic measures and ratios and they functioned as huge astronomical clocks aligned to the planets, predicting eclipses and verifying disputed measurements. These theories are founded on the notion that designers only require a method of representation if the appearance of the outcome is of importance. The more we uncover about the design approaches of the ancients, the more we find they were concerned less with appearance than with responses to esoteric and cabalistic figures. Concern for the visual appearance of buildings in anything other than applied decoration seems to have arisen only when aesthetics became a subject separate from metaphysics and philosophical speculation, and builders addressed themselves to the visual, the subjective and the fashionable. It is almost certain, therefore, that before pleasing their own aesthetic sensibilities, the Egyptians, Greeks and Romans built in relation to their sacred canons.

This is supported by the archaeologist, J.J. Coulton, who suggests that it is unlikely that Ancient Greek designers produced scale drawings of the plans and elevations of their temples because, within a technology lacking fine calibration, drawings in scale for such massive structures would have led to inaccuracies in their construction. A striving for precision in the widespread repetition of architectural components and buildings appears to have been more important to their visualization of space and form than any relationship to the immediate environment. This contrasts with the sentiments of Vitruvius who wrote: 'The look of a building when seen close at hand is one thing, on a height it is another, not the same in an enclosed space, still different in the open.' However, in suggesting that designs should be adjusted accordingly Vitruvius was referring to Roman buildings which were often designed through a use of scale models; Greek

temples, on the other hand, being erected in isolation and on artificially levelled platforms, were never controlled by the nature of
their settings (fig. 2.)

If it is accepted that the Greek architect designed against proven
proportional systems (for these existed long before their philosophical theories had been elaborated by the Pythagoreans) it is
likely that rules were formulated in such a way that they were
'portable', being applied as buildings went up, with little detailed
design beforehand. If preliminary drawings were used at all,
Coulton suggests, it is more likely that they were for smaller parts
of buildings, for there is considerable evidence of a widespread
use of only *paradeigmata*, full-scale specimens of the more elaborate elements such as capitals. From these mock-ups builders
could extract detailed dimensions with callipers, thereby achieving
repetition from replicas without any need for scaling up or conver-
sions. However, intriguing accounts of a developing sophistication
in graphic representation in the Hellenistic period are to be found
in the writings of ancient commentators such as Democritus and,
later, Vitruvius. As part of the evolution of the accurately drawn
plan and elevation, they describe an innovation called
'skenography', a method of creating illusions of depth which was

**Fig. 2: Doric temple on an artificially
levelled site, Segesta, Sicily. Photo
William Taylor**

used in fourth century Greek theatre stage sets. This method was also described in a book written by Anaxagoras, itself in turn based on the practical experiments of the scenic artist Agartharchus. According to the commentators, skenography was later developed into a form of perspective drawing called 'aktinography' the mechanics of which have since been mysteriously lost to civilization. Its existence is also mentioned by Plutarch who, in connecting Agartharchus' achievement with its adoption by architects such as Pheidias, describes the consequent increase in the speed with which buildings - such as the Parthenon - were raised.

Vitruvius explains that, being related to the curvature of the eyeball and that of the earth, aktinography was a spherical rather than linear perspective - his justification being the entasis in the columns of the Parthenon and other temples (fig. 3). This implies a use of preliminary perspective drawings, for the design of such curves (to remove the optical effect of dead-weight and reduce the visual imbalance of an overhanging entablature) involves a mastery of freehand drawing. In any event, the Greeks' understanding of perception evidenced by their subtle modification of buildings is unequalled, even by a modern environment which is riddled with optical illusions. What is of interest, however, is that the design of the Parthenon might have been influenced, at least in part, by an artist's discovery.

Plans, as such, were not used in the design of western European architecture until the rediscovery of Euclidean geometry in 1100 AD. Without this geometry the forms of Gothic cathedrals would not have been possible because for the first time medieval architects, being committed to the Pythagorean concept of 'all is number', were able to set out accurately a plan against a network of repeated units and, again by modular geometry, project sections and elevations.

Fig. 3: Optically corrected columns on the temple of Hera at Paestum, Italy. Photo Max Hirmer

From th...
repre...
arch...
Ac... ...e of
d... ...se
w... ...erting a
variety o... ...example,
medieval archit... ...ient counterparts, enjoyed a pr... ...cause they
worked directly in space. The... ...ree-dimen-
sional concepts of potential buildi... ...ctural forms
contained within the library of the existi... environment, using other buildings as full-size models or specimens which could
be studied and then modified or refined. As artists in their own
right and with a practical knowledge of materials and construction, they were able to utilize design aids such as modular
geometry and drawing instruments much the same as those in
use today. When they employed a drawing it was often executed
to large or even fullsize on tracing-boards or on a specially pre-
pared plaster screed floor. It was only for smallscale details that
they drew on vellum on a trestle-board - the precursor of the
modern drawing-board.

Discounting the common claim that designers in the Middle Ages
used few, if any, design drawings, J. Harvey, in his account of medieval building, offers several arguments to explain why so few
have survived. He suggests that beyond their immediate utility
there was little reason for the architect to retain them; that the
large tracing-boards and plaster screed tablets were rubbed out,
and that parchment was such a valuable commodity that it was
recycled for other uses such as bookbinding. Indeed, several architectural drawings have been found concealed on the obverse
of medieval book covers. Perhaps his strongest argument is that
design techniques were considered to be secret and such secrets
were well concealed within the Guild societies. An illustration of

the lengths the Guilds would go in order to protect their secrets is found in the unfortunate killing of Bishop Conrad in 1099. He was assassinated by a zealous master mason who had learned that the Bishop's curiosity had unwittingly uncovered a secret method for waterproofing the foundations of St. Mary's Church in Utrecht, the Bishop's own church. However, some plan and elevation drawings do exist. Among the earliest known are those preserved in the 1335 sketchbook of the French architect Villard de Honnecourt (fig. 4).

The influx of Greek ideas into medieval draftsmanship simply sharpened the experiential skills of the vernacular builders who had, hitherto, developed an architecture in which a representational method was not necessarily a prerequisite of construction. In this traditional context the 'designer' was the builder, an artisan directly in control of building operations. Spatial concepts were carried completely within the 'mind's eye,' the architectural vocabulary evolving along a trial and error basis, but being directly linked to natural conditions and measured against anthropometric needs. Superimposed against this profound comprehension of space the architect-craftsperson emerges from the ranks of the builder-artisan, pausing during construction to translate concepts into crude plans and incomplete, fragmented elevations. But drawings of entire buildings were not made, perhaps just for lack of technical skill. The spontaneity with which the great Gothic churches spring up against gravity and the sky suggests they were never fully put down on paper. They arose unforeseen.

Thus the Gothic architect worked within a comparatively safe and familiar architectural style until 1284, when the roof fell in on his attempts to defy gravity with the collapse of Beauvais Cathedral. Until then the whole appearance of buildings had not been of prime importance for, even as late as 1301, the vaults of Milan Cathedral - felt to be too steep by a cautionary Commission - were modified through a mathematical approximation of Pythagorean

Fig. 4: Medieval attempt to describe orthographically two elevations of the towers of Laon cathedral. Page from Villard de Honnecourt's 1335 sketchbook.

triangles. A divine proportion was what was sought, and into that equation neither visual appearance nor the weight of stone ultimately entered.

Until well into the Middle Ages, architectural space was developed in this way; the medieval architect would take long journeys - even travelling abroad - in order to study and measure the essential proportions of 'full-sized specimens,' buildings which had been admired and selected by his patron for adaptation. The later introduction of a wooden scale model served only to communicate his intentions to the client and also extract a detailed estimate of cost. By the end of the Gothic period models of parts of buildings were being made, possibly for testing purposes. One form of model-making used as a design tool was the paper cut-out, which could demonstrate patterns of vaulting ribs and be bent by the medieval designer in order to simulate the intended structure of a space.

By contrast, his Renaissance counterpart had no such sure frame of reference as he was bent on an architecture inspired by a rubble of Graeco-Roman components, the apparent success of which was to provide a design-kit *par excellence* for the next five centuries. The only way he could test out the feasibility of these more dynamic visions was to build working models, sometimes in the actual materials he intended to use. It was, therefore, common practice to develop architectural concepts in the round by constructing large prefabrications in wood, clay or stone. These were not used purely for structural experiment as in the Middle Ages, but as design aids in the visual orchestration of mass and space. For example, Filippo Brunelleschi primarily invented in three dimensions and sometimes built his preparatory constructions to one twelfth of their proposed scale. Leon Battista Alberti's *Ten Books on Architecture* contains a description of the type of model he found useful in his design process. He writes: 'I would not have the model too exactly finished, not too delicate and neat, but plain and simple - more to be admired for the contrivance of the inventor than the hand of the workman.' Michelangelo also prefabricated full-sized wooden models of parts of his buildings as a visual check and, in a letter to Vasari complaining of an error which had developed during the erection of one project, he explained that it had arisen, '... even though I had made an exact model, as I always do'. Vasari also documented Michelangelo's design sequence for the cupola of St. Peter's in Rome which began with a clay model along with plan and section sketches; this initial phase led to the construction of a large wooden model (which took one year to complete) through which its final form was achieved (fig. 5).

The most significant event during the Renaissance was a development in the pictorial representation of space. Earlier attempts to organize the recession of planes into graphic illusions of depth through crude isometric and axonometric projection (sometimes in combination with plan views) can be found in ceramic and wall painting from the Greek period onwards. But the invention (or rediscovery from Arab mathematicians such as al-Khazen) of perspective marked a crucial turning point. Designers suddenly realized that they could translate their visual perceptions into an apparently comprehensible and manipulative series of delineated spatial events, capable of accurately rendering a design intention. Together with the evolution of the related plan and elevation, linear perspective was a further projection of the geometry which was at the essence of the ancient design philosophy. Although al-Khazen's treatise on perspective - which recognized that we see an object because each point of it directs a ray into the eye - was annotated in Latin by Lorenzo Ghiberti, it was Brunelleschi who first pioneered its practicability in two perspective panels (now lost) in 1417. Antonio du Tucci Manetti is attributed with the earliest documentation of the invention which he tells us was made in a drawing of a view across the Piazza del Duomo, Florence. Manetti describes Brunelleschi peeping from the back of one of

Fig. 5: A replica of Michelangelo's large scale preparatory wooden model for the cupola of St. Peter's in Rome. Courtesy Musei Vaticani

his panels through a hole bored at its centre at a mirror held at arm's length. In this fashion, his viewpoint was controlled so as to coincide with the vanishing point of the reflected picture image (fig. 6). Manetti also describes a second attempt made in the Piazza of the Palazzo dei Signori in which Brunelleschi covered the area above his drawn buildings with burnished silver. When this perspective was viewed in the mirror through the peephole, the drawn image combined with that of a reflected, natural sky.

However, the Renaissance literature that documents the invention raises several questions both as to the venue and the method of its innovation. Firstly, although biographers such as Manetti and Vasari agree that Brunelleschi's initial experiment recorded a view of the baptistry of San Giovanni seen from the doorway of the Cathedral of Santa Maria del Fiore, it is unlikely that he would have selected this subject, since just a few years previously Brunelleschi had lost the competition to design the bronze Baptistry doors to his arch-rival Ghiberti. A second question also concerns the position from which he is reported to have made the perspective drawing. If Manetti's estimation is accurate, more recent calculations show that Brunelleschi could not have clearly seen the view he is believed to have drawn. Indeed, it is thought that a building, since demolished, stood in the line of his view but with one of its windows coinciding with the assumed direction of his gaze. If so, this raises the possibility that the first perspective drawing was simply traced on glass. However, in fairness to these theories, it is not always easy to pinpoint precisely the exact position from which a building is painted.

Suspicions are also aroused at the disparity between the accounts of Manetti and Vasari together with the fact that Alberti - although accrediting Brunelleschi with the discovery in *Della Pittura* - did not describe its geometry. By contrast to Manetti's account of the use of mirrors and peep-holes, Vasari writes that his perspective was achieved in an 'unaided' manner, being geometrically

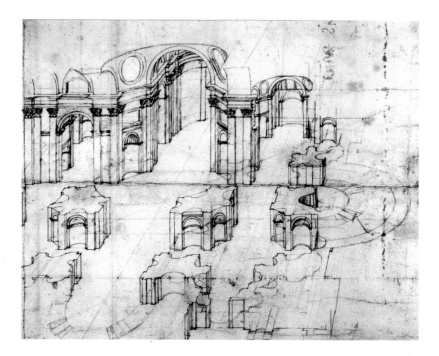

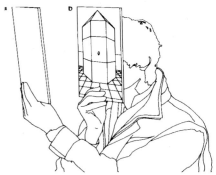

Fig. 6: (below) Brunelleschi's two-panel system for viewing a perspective drawing. Courtesy Kevin Forseth.
Fig. 7: (left) Drawing of St. Peter's, Rome by Baldassare Peruzzi. This remarkable synthesis of plan, section, perspective and horizontal section combines, for the first time, the abstract nature of orthographics with the subjective character of perspective.

constructed by tracing the intersecting lines between ground plan and elevation. Furthermore, Brunelleschi himself might have perpetuated the confusion when, in supporting his claim to have invented perspective, he exhibited his two panels possibly without any explanation of their geometry. This medieval-like secrecy would have been in keeping with his character for he is reported to have advised: 'do not share inventions with the many.'

One interest Brunelleschi did share with his contemporaries was a fascination for sundial technology which, incidentally, functions using coordinates inherent in perspective drawing. This analogy between viewpoint/picture plane relationships in perspective and gnomon/scale relationships in sundials gives rise to some interesting speculation. If Brunelleschi had used mirrors, a far more elegant solution to his problem would have been to fit a horizontal gnomon into a hole at the centre of a silvered panel. This procedure would avoid the intrusion of his own reflection and allow him to stand back and align his sight with the point of the gnomon and the mirror image of the selected view. Then, removing the gnomon, he could peep through its socket from the back to a further mirrored image of his drawing and experience an

Fig. 8: Perspective at work: a constructed cityscape from Vriedman de Vries, *On Perspective*, 1599

unreversed, single-point perspective. Enthusiasm for this invention concretized into an identifiable school of *perspectivi*. Early paintings which employed perspective, such as Masaccio's frescos for the Brancacci Chapel in Florence, had holes drilled at their centre which, it is assumed, held a peg from which strings could be attached for marking the vanishing lines. Linear perspective was first applied to the delineation of building designs by Donato Bramante and Baldassare Peruzzi approximately 50 years later (fig. 7). The eventual access to perspective meant that architects could now make accurate graphic overtures of an as-yet unbuilt 'architecture of the mind', and show them within their settings (fig. 8). This newfound skill was developed and improved until three hundred years later it achieved a high-point in the fantastic compositions of master draftsmen such as Piranesi.

The penetration of space through Brunelleschi's delineation positioned the architect outside his concept by placing distance between the viewer and the viewed - the very word 'per-spective' means through-seeing, which refers to the drawing as a window or, in the Ancient Greek version, a stage-set. This conceptual stance of looking into or at a two-dimensional illusion of space had not been the case in pictorial treatments of all cultures. For instance, in oriental art vanishing lines radiated away from the spectator into a wider concept of space - a reversed perspective which, in positioning the mind's eye behind the picture plane, allowed the artist to visualize from 'inside' the concept. Brunelleschi's perspective was a contradiction to the very nature of visual perception as it caused the viewer to freeze in time and space. Its inherent symmetry and straightness resulted from the static, central viewpoint which, together with a pure linear dissection of the picture plane, became absorbed into Renaissance architecture's search for an ideal geometrical unity.

Glass, first discovered by the Egyptians, was another technology that was to further the movement towards humanism during the early Renaissance as it was to affect concepts of spatial visualization. Lewis Mumford, indeed, has described the transition between the philosophies of the medieval and Renaissance periods in terms of the gradual purification and subsequent clarification of window glass. Medieval symbolism, represented by the brightly coloured stained-glass of cathedral windows began to dissolve into the clear glass of the fourteenth century, allowing an unimpeded view through to the form and colours of nature, a naturalistic perception characteristic of the beginning of new thought in Europe. A new and sharply focused world was also framed by the glass of spectacles which, in adding additional years to eyesight, had boosted the revival of learning. By the sixteenth century the invention of the microscope and the simultaneous improvements of telescopic optics had, on the one hand, rocketed the vanishing point into outer space and towards infinity; on the other, in the words of Mumford, it had 'increased almost infinitely the plane of the foreground from which those lines had their point of origin'. In this way, Mumford explains that glass had shattered man's naive conceptions of space and extended his perception of an expanding world. However, a world viewed through the glass of windows, spectacles and optical instruments is a framed perception - the very impression reinforced by the parallel development of linear perspective.

As the architect began to shed his creative dialogue with three dimensions and work almost entirely with graphic means, the model began to assume a different role. By the seventeenth century it had become an explanatory device rather than an exploratory tool. For example, Sir Christopher Wren considered the model to be less for his own benefit than for that of builders or client. He wrote that 'a good and careful large model' should be constructed for ' the encouragement and satisfaction of the benefactors who comprehend not designs and drafts on paper.' As an adjunct to a visualization process in which drawing had become a language of the initiated, the new role of model-making represented a further step away from any holistic conceptualization of space. This shift of emphasis was reflected in the high degree of finish of models and was synchronous with a movement towards the communication of external appearance for its own sake.

By the mid-nineteenth century the refinement of another drawing system came to emphasize drawing as the central means of architectural design. Initially classified as top secret by the French government, the development of a means of graphically showing a standardized and precise viewing relationship between the upper, side and front views of a complex object, by the physicist and military engineer Gaspard Monge, was to have a profound impact on visualization techniques. Despite this initial censorship, Monge's orthographic system - known as 'First Angle Projection' - provided a means of coordinating the plan with elevation and the section, and quickly became common currency in both architectural and engineering circles. Indeed, it had been devised in time to serve the accurate delineation of new inventions such as Stephenson's steam-powered Rocket locomotive and Brunel's complex machinery, among the many inventions which emerged during the Industrial Revolution (figs. 9 & 10).

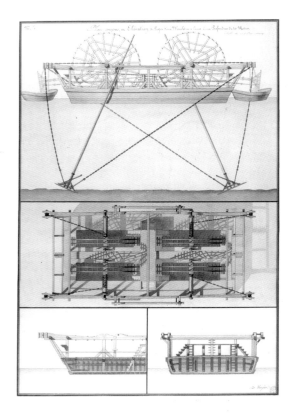

Fig. 9: Orthographic drawing was an essential element in the creation of the Industrial Revolution, as in this French 1819 drawing for a dredger. Courtesy Ecole Nationale des Ponts et Chaussées.

Another significant landmark was also to occur at the turn of the nineteenth century - the institutionalization of the architectural profession and the formalizing of architectural education. This event heralded a growing concern for fine-line drafting skills in which technical drawing was considered to be tantamount to an art form. Aesthetically, the architect became less concerned with the sculptural qualities of form and space and instead turned to designing in terms of the pictorial nature of facade and silhouette and, in communicating these concepts to others, even the 'presentation model' was to be superseded for a time by the ubiquitous 'artist's impression'. Also, the growth of the print medium encouraged a proliferation of ideas through journals, which had meant that by 1900 drawing had finally become the acceptable language of the architect.

This obsession with drafting techniques and beautiful drawings was to survive a series of broadsides over the years from such theorists as John Ruskin, William Morris, and later Henry Van de Velde and Walter Gropius. The attacks came at a time when design schools such as the Ecole des Beaux Arts were extolling virtuoso draftsmanship as the key to architectural elegance. In rebelling against the remoteness of paper designs from the real world of work, Gropius founded the Bauhaus in 1919 and devised its revolutionary curriculum in the hope of resurrecting the medieval 'lost chord' between designer and craftsman. Although its programme included the study of plane geometry and drafting techniques one tutor, Laszlo Moholy-Nagy - a Constructivist with a predilection for the dynamics of light - encouraged his students to employ as a design tool a simple, partly transparent model which he called a 'space modulator'. He explained that this was intended to provide them with an opportunity of relating concepts to materials 'as against previous architectural methods in which structural inventions were hampered by the shortcomings of visualization on paper alone'.

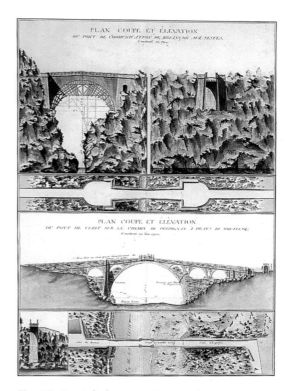

Fig. 10: Partial plans, sections and elevations for the Pont d'Asfeld, 1734, and the fourteenth-century Pont de Céret, published by Perronet in 1794. Courtesy Ecole Nationale des Ponts et Chaussées.

Linear perspective was completely abandoned in the early twentieth century by the Cubist painters who, influenced by Cézanne's perceptual rationale of form, Kepler's cine-camera and primitive African abstractions of space, experimented with the portrayal of the whole structure of any given object and its position in space (fig. 11). Cubism, contemporaneous with Einstein's theories, introduced the concept of time into art, and Picasso's experiments with the dynamic interpretation of transparent planes brought a new sensibility of space in terms of our trajectory through it. Picasso's preoccupation with the totality of perception influenced architects such as Gropius and Le Corbusier to reject the perspective as limited, finite and closed and to adopt for completeness the axonometric drawing - a characteristically cubic diagram which induces its user to assume a hovering, almost godlike view of the architect's conception. As opposed to linear perspective which encourages looking through and up at the interiors and exteriors of architectural space, the axonometric pushes the viewer's stance upwards, causing the visual erosion of the corners of buildings (fig. 12). It is interesting to note that the researches of the artists Agartharchus, Brunelleschi and Picasso into models of spatial representation had, at respective points in time, influenced the articulation of built environment - the last affecting a post-1920 architecture in which both exterior and interior are simultaneously visible in a transparency of layered and floating glassy planes.

In this context of relating representational methods to the appearance of architecture, it is worth mentioning the design approach of Antoni Gaudí, a designer of unquestionable genius whose visualization methods were as unconventional as his architectural forms. His designs for the Church at Santa Coloma and the Sagrada Familia in Barcelona did not include graphic techniques but were evolved through a series of inverted wire and canvas models, worked out with the engineer Eduardo Goetz, and the sculptor Bertran. He rarely drew plans and relied almost

Fig. 11: Georges Braque: *Oval Still Life (Le Violon),* oil on canvas. Private collection.

exclusively upon three-dimensional forms of visualization - a method which rather than inhibiting creativity, increased his capacity for articulating highly complex space. Gaudí's grasp of space was reinforced by workshop experience and a feel for materials which echoed that of the medieval architects.

It is this essential grasp which marks the important early twentieth century architects as creative designers who visualize and articulate spatial concepts in an imaginative and unconventional manner. A random study of their formative experience and design methods discloses a conceptual process which, being founded upon an understanding of the potential of space in all its manifestations, transcends a singular reliance upon drawing. For example, in the book *Eero Saarinen on His Own Work*, he describes his own visualization process which replicates that of Michelangelo by first modelling space in clay before any graphic interpretation. Saarinen explains that the plasticity of the form of his TWA terminal in New York's JFK Airport could not have been achieved on paper alone. A break with the rigidity of graphics we associate with traditional drafting is embodied in the highly expressive drawings of Eric Mendelsohn and Louis Kahn. Le Corbusier, like his Renaissance counterpart, was an artist in his own right, although he only had the use of one eye: as part of his Venice Hospital Project, he drew to full-size an exploratory section through a ward space on his studio blackboard as a means of judging its implications as realistically as possible. Meanwhile, in adopting a more sculptural approach, Luigi Nervi's concrete forms have remained fluid beyond the drawing-board by being subjected to a medieval-like modification during the course of their construction.

However, in tracing the shifting roles of three- and two-dimensional models of visualization along broader spectrums we find that, after 1920, the Modern Movement's rejection of a Beaux Arts academism had paralleled a revival in the use of scale models.

Fig. 12: The popularity of rotating the plan for its upward projection into an axonometric, such as in Gropius' Fagus Factory and here on the Bauhaus workshop wing in Dessau, might have caused the visual erosion of the corners of the building. Courtesy Bauhausarchiv.

These were enlisted for the three-dimensional 'sketching' of a purist and uncluttered space. Such white cardboard models miniaturized, presented and proliferated the new International Style - causing the model-maker's craft to be mirrored in a built architecture stripped of ornamentation. However, the current obsession with drawing stems from the 1960s which saw the formation of design groups akin to the grouping of ideologies amongst Renaissance artists. Such groups include the influential Archigram who explored a speculative science-fiction aesthetic using brightly coloured Pantone film to zone and differentiate functional areas in their machine-like delineations. Their use of Pantone became an end in itself and was later to influence the colour-coded appearance of an ensuing high-tech architecture in the 1970s. Another group known as the New York Five also influenced the trend toward exquisitely and clinically delineated plans and projections. One of its members, Michael Graves, became identified later with a post-Modernist movement to restore the elaboration of a Beaux Arts approach. During the 1970s and 1980s, architectural drawing went beyond the level of a window on the design process and became elevated to the status of a work of art, exhibited on the international art market.

Three thousand years after the first known architectural drawing was made in Memphis, Egypt, the act of drawing remains central to the act of designing habitable space. Indeed it would be difficult to name any internationally recognized architect without making a mental reference to their drawing style. Style of drawing is associated with individuality; a kind of personal signature that instantly identifies the architect and the design philosophy. Furthermore, many architects, such as Peter Eisenman, had established themselves by producing a 'paper architecture' well before they became involved in construction. For instance, one such designer whose widely published drawings and paintings have, until recently, featured an unbuilt architecture is Zaha Hadid (see page 93). Influenced more by the dynamism of a Russian

Fig. 13: In abandoning pictorial modes Daniel Libeskind's *Chamberworks* **explore ideas using spatial signs to be deciphered rather like a musical score.**

Suprematist vision than by a conventional perspective, her images employ different sets of vanishing points within a single format, each controlling different zones of the painting. Consequently, their multi-angled viewpoints cause our perception to animate; at one moment we hover in space; at another moment we are, seemingly, sweeping past at warp speed. Her drawings and paintings are activated by a distinctive layering technique that involves a clearly defined and tensioned orchestration of angular and gently curving planes.

In conjunction with John Lyall, the majority of the British architect Will Alsop's early work existed only in drawn and painted form (see page 92). However, his later transition to a built architecture still sees his initial investigation of architectural ideas as expressed in large acrylic canvases. These paintings explore embryonic concepts in terms of form, shape and colour, the architectural idea emerging from the sheer liquidity of the acrylic medium. Another architect who has made the transition from paper to built architecture is Daniel Libeskind, whose early work, like Eisenman's, was to reappraise conventional architectural representation. He abandoned accepted pictorial modes in favour of an intensely private language of spatial signs and symbols intended to be deciphered rather like musical scores. Libeskind's 'Chamberworks' (fig. 13) and 'Micromegas' (fig. 14) are suites of drawings which present a fluctuating graphic field, with each image in the sequence tracing the route of his continually changing thinking process. By employing signs, lines and accents, his drawings not only established the platform of his ensuing buildings but transcend the everyday function of architectural graphics. They disclose a mutating and liberating abstract geometry, while taking on a kind of poetic, textual dimension which takes us to the very origins of Deconstruction.

From this short survey of the design of space and the changing interaction of two and three dimensions in its articulation it

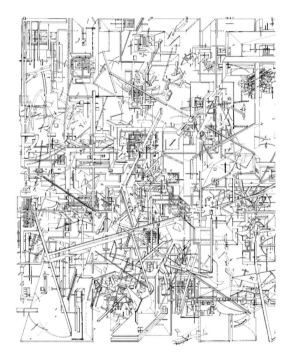

Fig. 14: Daniel Libeskind: Micromega
The Burrow Laws, **composite drawing, silkscreen on paper**

should be clear that, since the Renaissance, the architect has gradually developed away from direct spatial manipulation and, instead, increasingly invested in graphic interpretations of ideas. This emphasis on drawing, either as an enrichment or reduction of architectural concepts or as a convenient vehicle for spatial codes, has been in use for around 3,000 years, but has been at the centre of architectural education particularly in recent decades. This places a tremendous responsibility on the young designer to understand the implications both of the limitations and creative potential that drawing can have on spatial thinking. Too often, the student imitates graphic conventions such as the 'non-spatial' languages originally devised to communicate purely dimensional information to the builder without exploring alternative avenues of expression.

With the inherent dangers of this situation, the need to understand the spatial potential of drawing - in its many forms - is paramount: as a means of creating feedback from spatial experience, as a vehicle for quickly exploring ideas, and, in context with other modes of representation, as a dialogue between three and two dimensions.

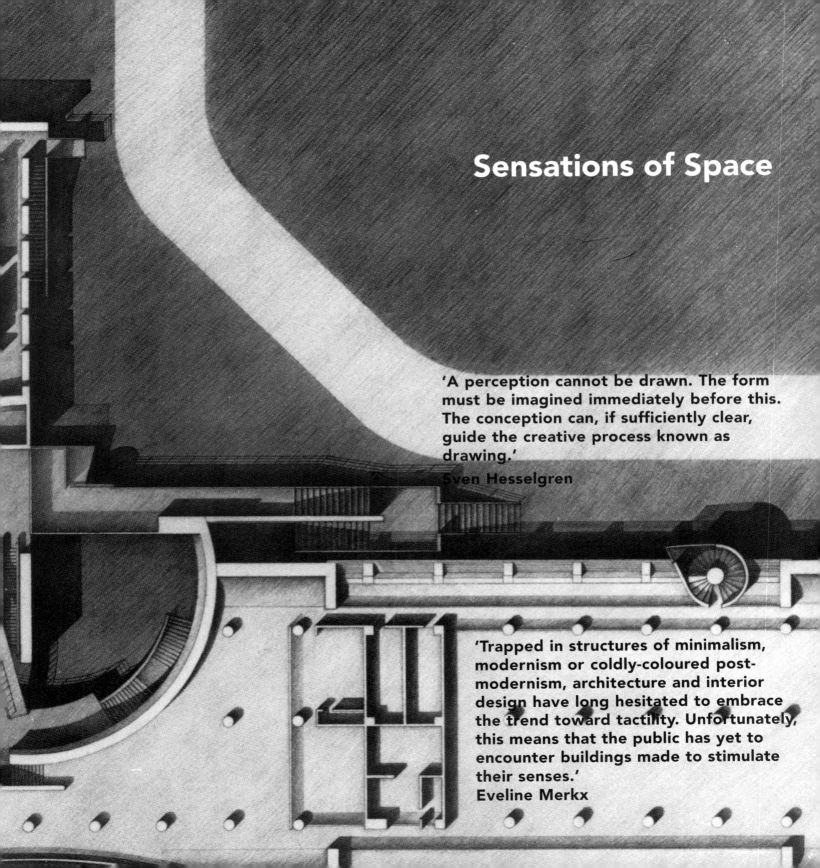

Sensations of Space

'A perception cannot be drawn. The form
must be imagined immediately before this.
The conception can, if sufficiently clear,
guide the creative process known as
drawing.'
Sven Hesselgren

'Trapped in structures of minimalism,
modernism or coldly-coloured postmodernism, architecture and interior
design have long hesitated to embrace
the trend toward tactility. Unfortunately,
this means that the public has yet to
encounter buildings made to stimulate
their senses.'
Eveline Merkx

Sensations of Space

Within design education philosophies concepts of space and form are usually separated and regarded respectively as the negative and positive of the physical world, a world where solid objects reside and where the void - the mere absence of substance - is a surrounding atmospheric emptiness. However, since the beginning of the nineteenth century, there has been an alternative concept of space as a continuum, as the continuously modified surface skin between the pressures of form and space in which the shape of the space in our lungs is directly connected to the shape of the space within which we exist (which is, in turn, just a layer of the space surrounding our planet). Architecture, therefore, can be considered as a creative expression of the coexistence of space and form on a human scale but its understanding, together with all other concepts, is rooted in the psychological space of our thoughts. Meanwhile, as a consequence of experimental psychology studies, space has become more dynamic and 'tangible'. As a result of attempts to understand the mechanics of perception, research findings begin to inform the designer about the nature of its many forms. The central issue of this chapter is the need to develop an awareness of the 'form of space' as an element vital in itself. In examining various concepts of space, it is intended to encourage what is lacking in contemporary design procedures - the essential grasp of space.

Architecture as Space

Our perceived experience of interior and exterior architectural space is primarily a sensual event involving movement - for to pass through an environment is to cause a kaleidoscope of transitions between one spatial impression and another. Each experience affects the orchestrated functioning of our senses in a variety of ways - our eyes, ears, nose and skin registering changing stimuli which trigger a flood of brain responses on all levels. For example, a visit to a funfair or theme park can provide a gamut of heightened response through unusual and extreme sensations of space. Helter-skelter, carousel and roller-coaster offer exhilarating opportunities to spiral, spin and undulate through space at speed, literally breathtaking experiences. The fairground environment is also filled with exaggerated levels of sound, smell, taste, and touch together with amplified volumes of form and colour for 'all the fun of the fair'. By contrast, to enter a medieval cathedral is to leave behind the sights, sounds and smells of the hubbub outside and to replace them with a new range of sensations monitored by our body. The skin registers a reduction in temperature, the eyes accommodate both the lower levels of light and the intense coloured light from stained-glass windows, the nose detects musty and sometimes mysterious, exotic odours and the ears pick up the echoes of isolated, reverberating sounds against the concentrated stillness of a vast, cavernous space.

The richness of spatial diversity is all around us in the natural and built environment and, indeed, in relationships between the two. We can experience unlimited space from vantage points on high ground and tall buildings, partially defined space from within canyons and streets, and totally enclosed space from inside the scooped-out depths of caves and subways or from within the confines of windowless rooms such as elevators. When revealed along a continuous viewing route, successive spatial diversity can exhilarate the human organism. Movement from restricted to expansive space, and vice versa, by their contrast seems to make the experience more impressive; this search for contrast accounts for our fascination for the funnelled approach to piazzas and the spatial confinement and release encountered in Greek island villages and in Italian hill towns (figs15 & 16). Each experience is modified by the prevailing conditions under which it is perceived, be it midday light or dusk, rain, snow or fog. As a facet of this experience, architectural space is subject to a whole series of perceptual overlays: day-night and seasonal cycles which cause it to be illuminated alternately by light from the sun, by its reflected light from the moon, and by artificial light sources - the degree of lightness or darkness influencing our perception of spaciousness.

Figs 15 & 16: Spatial contraction and release are classic architectural devices: the standpoint for these two images is the same, but the camera has turned through 180 degrees.

Also, depending upon its climatic setting, it is subject to periods of warmth or cold and changing air pressures. We could experience architectural space as a kaleidoscope of kinetics teeming with darting shadows, racing clouds, fluttering flags, the rise and fall of colour saturation, vibrations of growth and decay and, the essential ingredient, milling human beings living out their lives. The dynamism of this concept is generated by our movement about a vast global time-machine which is actually travelling at approximately 1,000 miles per hour - the speed at which the surface of our planet spins in space as it follows its endless orbit around the sun.

Perceptual Space

As we move through space each body, head and eye movement sets the visual environment in motion. We can look up, down and sideways and collect information even at the periphery of our field of vision; we can adjust by focusing on points in the far distance and points near at hand. The eyes receive spatial information which is, both in frequency and velocity, far in excess of that received by any other of the sense organs. The centre of visual attention in the eye, the foveal area, gathers information about shape and pattern by making many rapid eye fixations - a process which literally 'paints-in' a reconstruction of given stimuli. The surrounding peripheral retina gathers less detailed information and is sensitive to sudden changes in the environment, often signalling to the central focusing system to change the direction of focus.

Consequently, when we look at a scene, the eye cannot focus on more than one very small point at any one time. This tiny point of acuity sits at the centre of the much wider field of vision. Visual data from outside the focused centre becomes progressively less determinate as it ranges out to the blurred outer reaches of our peripheral vision. Therefore, a scene is never viewed 'at a glance' - rather, it is reconstructed via a scanning sequence in which the eye flits continuously from point to point to complete an almost instantaneous visual reconnaissance of the situation. This visual scanning process is an issue-orientated operation, and so people with quite different motives and interests will view the same scene in quite different ways. The physiology of the brain indicates that the focal and peripheral visual systems operate in parallel using different processing centres, and that our visual scanning process is capable of monitoring up to 30 separate images every second. Despite the importance of vision we should never ignore the involvement of the other distance receptors: hearing in relation to the acoustic properties of space, and smell in aiding identification and orientation; the immediate receptors (skin, membranes and muscles) being more subtle in their sensitivity to the ambient temperature, humidity, texture and shape. The combination of these varied sensory inputs reinforces, elaborates and may even alter our visual perception of the environment to give us a complete image which, in turn, can be modified by our own personality and motivation.

Much of our understanding of environment is experienced through the sense of touch yet, except when the more radical aspects of physical comfort and discomfort are involved, there is probably little conscious awareness on your part of the sensation of handling this book, the chair on which you now sit, or the support on which your elbows rest. As designers, our articulation of space could be far richer if we became only slightly more aware of the tactile sense.

One method of fine-tuning concentration on tactile experience is to close your eyes - a dampening down of the visual sense is often unconsciously used as a means of gaining heightened response to the other senses such as when listening to music or lovemaking. Similarly, a hungry person will screen-off other senses to enable food to be found, using a much more acute sense of smell. The American and European Colgate toothpaste 'ring of confidence' is a further example of screening or masking an olfactory space which, in an obsessively deodorised society embarrassed by bad breath, allows closer contact between people - some other peoples, however, accept body odours and can identify them with emotions. However, tactile and visual experiences are closely interwoven and, as experiments into sensory deprivation have shown, even though we can temporarily disconnect ourselves from sight, sounds, odours and tastes, we can never be free from tactile sensation for we have always the pressure of our body on the surface which supports it.

During the twentieth century perception has been considered as body centred, that is, our understanding of three-dimensional space emanates from information received through all our five senses. Some authors, such as J.J. Gibson, suggest that basic orientating (the postural sense of up and down establishing our knowledge of the ground plane) and the haptic sense (the sense of touch involving the entire body) are the primary means through which we understand our sense of being. However, from an architectural standpoint, Kent Bloomer and the late Charles Moore have suggested that the incorporation of a body-centred view of space in architectural design has been virtually eradicated this century in favour of a singularly visual approach. In *Body, Memory and Architecture* they write: 'The historic overemphasis on seeing as the primary sensual activity in architecture necessarily leads us away from our bodies. This results in an architectural model which is not only experientially imbalanced but in danger of being restrictive and exclusive ... especially when we consider that all sensory activity is accompanied by a bodily reaction.'

Multi-sensory Space

In designing a house in up-state New York for a partially-sighted client, Charles Moore and his partner Richard B. Oliver undertook a project which had met with reluctance from other designers daunted by the thought that its user would never see the result. Since the blind live in a haptic world of surfaces, Moore and Oliver's response was to make something that could be felt as well as seen, and set out to produce an architecture which articulates texture, sound and smell to act as locational messages. For example, to obviate the use of air-conditioning - and its attendant stale odour - on all but the most oppressive days, the house incorporates a high-level window ventilation system. The client can actually smell from which direction a breeze is blowing by the fragrance it carries: from a pine forest on the north side of the house, or from the peach orchard to the south. Orientation around the house is further aided by sensations of controlled sunlight and shade on the skin and from the fragrances from an indoor garden and a conservatory containing several varieties of aromatic plants such as lemon trees (fig. 17).

In addition to olfactory clues, auditory messages are introduced in the form of a sunken indoor fountain whose splashing sound is enhanced musically by metal tuning forks embedded in its cascade. More subtly, Moore and Oliver included a series of rooms of varying size and proportion which, ingeniously functioning as sounding-chambers, reverberate ambient sounds from which their client can locate position. Furthermore, the point of entry to each room is signalled by small, uncarpeted areas so that the client's arrival and, indeed, the approach of others, is announced by the sound of footfalls. On the upper level, the oak planked and rug covered floors of rooms are connected by wall-to-wall carpeted corridors; ground floor circulation is paved with more adventurous and reverberant handmade terracotta quarry tiles. With its softened corners and varying underfoot textures, the circulation route twists and turns like an ancient street. This route

Fig. 17: Interior of the New York house designed for a partially-sighted client by Charles Moore and Richard B. Oliver. Photo Norman McGrath

Fig. 18: (facing) The interior of the upper gallery of Hiroshi Naito's Gallery Tom, Tokyo, showing the kinaesthetic use of sunlight and shade (see page 35)

Fig 19. (below) Another highly sensational interior in Nagasaki's Port Terminal Building by the architect Shin Takamatsu (see also pages 90 & 91) Courtesy Nacàsa & Partners.

incorporates a snaking mahogany guide rail with a profile that replicates one the client and his sighted wife had experienced and found extremely pleasurable during a stopover in a small Pennsylvania airport.

The architects' sensitivity to their client's special needs did not preclude the visual sense for, apart from the fact that the partially sighted are often peripherally sensitive to light and find direct light extremely distressing, sighted people also occupy the house. Consequently, the house is lit exclusively by the pervading and restful ambience of indirect light, but on several surfaces around the house it is complemented by a dazzling array of vari-egated ceramic tiles. Thus the client can enjoy the feel of their cool, smooth surface while delighting in their rich and highly con-trasting ranges of purples and greens - detected as a visual sensation near the outer edge of his visual field. It might also be argued that the architects' addressed all the five senses for, if the fruit grown in the orangery is edible, then the sense of taste can be added to those of touch, sound, sight and smell.

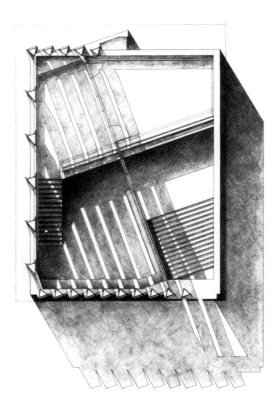

Although motivated by necessity, the sensory subtleties of this house emphasize one of the most significant omissions in con-temporary architecture. Namely, the need to design for all the senses. Indeed, Martin Filler underscores this need when he writes: 'Perhaps the most glaring fallacy in much of the neo-Pla-tonic architecture of the past half century has been the dangerous belief that a humanly satisfying building need not take more into consideration than proportional perfection or composi-tional purity. Many such buildings have attained their diagrammatic climax much more effectively in two dimensions than they ever have in three; but a house for real people with real bodies must account for much more'. In designing this house to be aurally, tactilely, aromatically and visually intelligible to its handicapped user, Moore and Oliver begin to point toward a multi-sensory architecture that could be of benefit to us all.

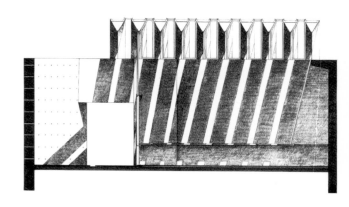

Their design also accentuates the kinaesthetic aspect of our tactile appreciation of space, space primarily perceived through the skin and muscles and in response to our position within or movement through it. Oriental designers are also particularly aware of the subtle relationships between visual and kinaesthetic space for, in a culture where living space is at a premium, they can stretch experience through a masterly manipulation of irregularly positioned textures and objects which necessitate an increased and correspondingly irregular number of muscular sensations.

Our bodily contact with the edges of space is central to our awareness of ourselves and our spatial location. It seems important, therefore, that as designers of environments we should base future built spaces upon some understanding of their contribution to the common attitude found in art galleries and museums where, in being politely discouraged from touching sculptural objects, we might be forgiven for believing that form and surface elaboration are something to be sensed purely through the eyes!

Figs 20-22: Plan (facing) exterior elevation (top) and section (above) for the Gallery Tom.

However, in Shibuya, a bustling shopping district of Tokyo, stands one art gallery in the world where visitors are positively encouraged to experience sculpture using the sense of touch (figs 18, 20-22). Here, for instance, one can caress a Rodin or make a tactile exploration of a Giacometti. This is the Gallery Tom - a touch-me art museum and performance space designed for a hands-on appreciation of sculpture for the blind and partially-sighted. Housed in a shell of crusty reinforced concrete, Gallery Tom is a further example of an architecture sensitive to our experience of temperature, texture and acoustics. The shape of the first floor performance space and gallery is defined by a constantly changing floorscape: from cushioned tatami to polished cedar wood. Echoing the dual symmetries of the plan's footprint - a diagonally sliced rectangle - this variegated underfoot experience has two functions: it helps locate dancers and singers when

Fig. 23: (facing) The opulent curves of the seating in Gaudi's Parc Guell, Barcelona offer a psychological choice to the extrovert and the introvert. Photo Richard Bryant, Arcaid.

Fig. 24: (below) Anthony Caro's 'sculpitecture,' *Halifax Steps* . Photo Susan Crowe.

used as a performance space and, when used as a gallery, heralds the position of freestanding sculptures to visitors. The upper floor provides a smaller, quieter gallery. Above this the castellated roof is pierced by a row of diagonal strips of clerestory ceiling lights. These create shafts of alternating cool and warm air which are sensed kinaesthetically when visitors move about the space (see page 32).

In describing Gallery Tom its architect, Hiroshi Naito, acknowledges that although visual sensation provides more information to the brain than do the other senses, a vast amount of knowledge is required to comprehend the substance of our setting. To be visually appreciated, architecture has traditionally been covered with various materials to adorn its surface but, in the non-visual world, this effect is completely lost. This is because the eyes of the blind are always attuned to the world we cannot see: 'They experience the building by the number of steps, by feeling the light on their skin, they touch the volume of space by sound.'

Gallery Tom houses a formidable body of work including artists such as Picasso, Brancusi and Le Corbusier. Augmented by sculpture moulded and cast by blind children and adults who attend the museum's workshops, the collection is selected to exploit the hands-on discovery of new textures and form, some warm from paper and wood, others cool in brass and steel. However, apart from those who use their hands to see, these sensations are also shared by the many sighted visitors who, for a singular focus on the tactile, are provided with special eye masks. Like the blind and the partially-sighted, they also visit the museum in great numbers to heighten the intense and erotic physical pleasure of touch; to delight in the tactile variables of the smooth, the rough, the elastic and the fibrous.

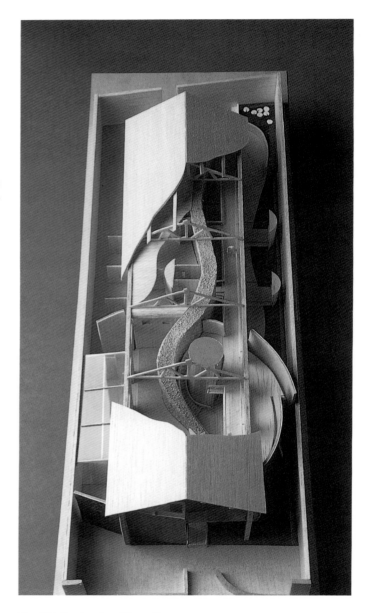

Fig. 25: Design by Alison Pearce for a Rehabilitation Centre for people with a visual impairment.

Projects which attempt an architecture intelligible to a wider sensory response, such as those by Moore and Oliver and by Naito, have inspired similar projects from students attending environmental design courses that offer such choices. One such project was undertaken by Alison Pearce at the Chelsea College of Art and Design, who now advises architects on the wider implications of multi-sensory design (fig. 25). Investigations into the potential of tactile, acoustic and kinaesthetic sensation in the built environment is also a facet of the Interior Architecture programme at Oxford Brookes University where, using three-dimensional and computer models, graduate architecture students explore the potential of a multi-sensory design language (fig. 26). There is also evidence that the act of making sculpture begins to move back toward the creation of an object in space that can be experienced by the hands and the body as well as by the eyes.

Anthony Caro is internationally regarded as Britain's leading modern abstract sculptor. During the 1990s, however, his work has undergone a kind of transformation; a shift resulting from his deep interest in the two enterprises of sculpture and architecture. Although these are separate disciplines, Caro sees them as sharing common aesthetic concerns (see page 37). For example, he describes the two activities as involving similar materials, a shared preoccupation with scale, form and space and a concern for the relationship of the viewer/user to the work. However, the architect's approach is more conceptual, by using a diminutive shorthand of small-scale drawings and models to work from the whole down to the particular. The sculptor, on the other hand, generally likes to think more directly, to work to actual size in the intended material and to employ a vision that can be perceptual and additive. Another comparison made by Caro refers to the end-product. For instance, a sculpture represents self-contained objects that exist both in and of themselves, and it embodies an edge, an 'invisible wall' that positions the spectator on the

Fig. 26: Design for a 'touch-me' museum project by Alex Upton, a student at Oxford Brookes University

Figs 27 & 28: Pannini's painted view of the Piazza Navona in Rome (top), compared with a photograph taken recently from a similar standpoint (below): see page 53. Courtesy Niedersachses Landesgalerie, Hanover.

Fig. 29 (facing): One of a series of chromolithographs produced in 1854 for Dickinson's *Comprehensive Pictures of the Great Exhibition of 1851*, which documents the impact of Owen Jones' colour system - complete with atmospheric haze - on the interior of the Crystal Palace (see page 52).

outside. Meanwhile, sculpture can defy gravity and fly free, while architecture remains firmly rooted to the ground, inviting us in - its conception moving outward from within.

Spurred on by the notion that sculpture and architecture can be nourished by each other, Caro's more recent works focus on the boundary between the two. Indeed, they explore the very point at which sculpture and architecture meet. He describes this erosion of disciplinary boundaries as a process of 'opening sculpture out', of wresting it from the world of objects. For instance, what was a visual hole now becomes an opening through which a person might physically squeeze to gain access to internal spaces. The bodily action of squeezing into and around his work is, he suggests, the physical equivalent of what is happening when we explore visually a piece of sculpture. Indeed, to intensify the sense of discovery Caro has tightened the 'entrances' of more recent works, in order to make them more awkward to negotiate. With titles such as 'Ziggurat and Spirals' and 'Halifax Steps' (see page 37), Caro's sculpture now extends to occupy almost the same space as that articulated by architects (fig. 30). To do so, these works assume a bigness but not a monumentality; they occupy human-scale space and interact both with the architecture that houses them and the people who engage with them. Furthermore, not only does his sculpture function at the interface between the architectural space it occupies and inner spaces it provides, it exists at the very frontiers of both disciplines.

Sometimes referred to as 'Sculpitecture', Caro's work points us to the rewards that may be gained from looking beyond the edge of our own disciplines. Having collaborated on one occasion with the Californian architect Frank O. Gehry, he glimpses the new possibilities of what might result when architects and sculptors begin to learn from each other.

Fig. 30: Anthony Caro's working model for *Lakeside Folly*, **1988, demonstrates his philosophy of a 'habitable' sculpture. Courtesy Annely Juda Fine Art.**

Perceptual-Psychological Space

Pioneer work by E.T. Hall and R. Sommer has re-evaluated our relationship with our spatial setting and demonstrated that our conception of space is by no means confined to the volume occupied by our bodies. We exhibit similarities with animals in that we carry with us various territories or bubbles of personal space which emanate from zealously guarded intimate zones and extend across private sectors to wider and less personal frontiers. Not only does this psychological space shrink and expand between personal and less exclusive parameters, but the concept of our own physical size can fluctuate in response to a psychological spatial relationship, our body seemingly growing in stature when confined in small spaces such as elevators and, conversely, diminishing within vast spaces such as cathedrals or auditoria.

The concept of non-physical space is moved to broader spectra with K. Lewin's theory of 'psychological life-space' and the notion of 'action space' proposed by Horton and Reynolds. Lewin's life-space refers to the perceptual map in which we live out our life span. At its core is our personal space (home, room and family) from which we journey along familiar spatial corridors for work, recreation and social contact. Extending this perceptual map are concepts of geographically distant space, its limits being electronically expanded by radio, telephone, television and, of course, the information superhighway. The theory of action-space attempts to relate behaviour, perception and sociocultural attitudes. We place self-imposed limits on our location and movement through space by decisions made within socioeconomic frameworks; decisions which dictate the location of our home, workplace and mode of travel, with additional factors such as length of residence influencing our perception of the urban environment. Such influences produce various forms of perceptual screening in different kinds of space. For instance, in a cathedral people will tend to move more slowly and speak only in whispers. In an overcrowded elevator an individual's perception of that space will be altered - just as a person experiencing a visually pleasant and thermally comfortable room 'sees' the space in a totally different fashion from someone occupying the same room with the heating increased to levels of discomfort. Kenneth Bayes has described two kinds of movements through space: 'one exploratory through an unknown environment; the other habitual through a known environment. In the first (called 'tourist') the architecture is new, prominent and strange; one is exploring, open and receptive, moving and experiencing new things, investigating. In the second (called 'habitué') the architecture is in the background, hardly noticed; one moves through it without the awareness of the surroundings, thinking only of a goal.'

Studies of the way we inhabit and behave in different public spatial settings provide fascinating insight for the environmental designer. For instance, there is our preference for making right turns rather than left turns when entering crowded rooms; there is our desire to sit at the edges of restaurant spaces - suggesting a desire to see without being too obvious to others. In public space the role of eye contact and body language on interpersonal distance has been the subject of studies by Michael Argyle and Desmond Morris which suggest a need for choice. A classic example of psychological choice in public space is exemplified in Anton Gaudí's serpentine seating in Barcelona's Parc Guell. Here, the configuration of its meandering plan presents a range of options for both the introvert and the extrovert (see page 36). For example, the former can find a secluded vantage point sitting deep within the recess of an empty bay, while the latter can pose at the peak of the curve and in direct eye contact with passers-by.

One aspect of our spatial experience is perceptual conditioning. Culturally, we live in a rectilinear world - a world of space defined by buildings and boxes characterised by straight lines and right-angled corners. Even the room-space you now occupy will be created from planes, objects and openings derived from squares and rectangles which have been transferred directly from the designer's drawing-board. An overexposure to this kind of environment has meant that our vision, being continually bombarded with rectilinear information, has, in a subtle way, developed a highly conditioned and specialized perception. A by-product of this conditioning is that our visual perception can be distorted to experience optical illusions. For example, during a visit to James Stirling's Olivetti Building in Surrey a group of young design students were asked to describe the plan of the roof above a ramped corridor (fig. 31). The majority believed that they were perceiving a parallel rectangle when, in fact, the plan was tapered. Such optical distortions are common in our perception of the modern environment, such as the apparent upward thickening of tall apartment blocks and, in two dimensions, our inability to read certain shapes as being flat.

In comparing primitive and sophisticated perceptions, R.L. Gregory describes the world of Zulu tribesmen, who have little use for corners or straight lines. Theirs is a curvilinear culture in which dome-shaped huts filled with rounded furniture and artifacts are entered through circular openings - an agricultural society of farmers who plough, not in straight lines, but in curves. Gregory explains they do not experience the optical illusions common to our perception. Other anthropologists, such as Andrew Forge, have also underlined our specialized vision by demonstrating that members of the Ablam tribe in New Guinea cannot read photographs. This inability to decipher two dimensional images of spatial events is based on the fact that they have not learned to interpret photographic imagery, being much more exposed to the natural environment. To this 'primitive' perception an environment filled with corners is an environment full of mysterious and useless adjuncts of space.

As a means of broadening our perceptual awareness it is, therefore, important that we immerse ourselves consciously in spatial

Fig. 31: Photograph of the ramp leading to the reception area in Stirling's Olivetti Building. Photo Mike Jenks

diversity, for our visual conditioning not only influences the formation, externalisation and development of ideas but predetermines the nature of a resulting architecture, which in turn conditions the perception of those who inhabit it.

Conceptual Space

As opposed to the psychological dimension of behavioural space and the tactility and measurability of physical space, conceptual space is that which we perceive and visualize. The design of space is, initially, a mental concept and any resultant response is primarily experienced through visual perception. However, a form-orientated approach to design is still prevalent, in which space can be literally ignored or, if considered, exist as a kind of waste-product after design. It is essential, therefore, that in tuning our mental attitude to the transfer of visual information a step is made across this conceptual threshold - from a form dominated perception to a renewed awareness of space as dynamic, tangible substance. This threshold can be traversed by conducting a simple experiment using the classic figure-ground model (fig. 32).

By fixing our vision on the central vase image as object we can apprehend the traditional conception of form in space where the contours defining the vase represent form-orientated thinking; the vase symbolizes an architecture of containment. However, if we psychologically switch off to a concentration on the outer areas (the two face profiles) we discover that the surrounding negative transforms into a positive but different entity which not only reflects the nature of the vase but takes on a life and meaning of its own. In our new perception, what was at first void has now become tangible - the vase to faces alternation causes a graphic experience of the concept of space as a dynamic presence, being redefined by the same contours which had previously described the vase. In returning to our analogy with architecture, we can begin to understand a positive concept of environmental

Fig. 32: Figure-ground model: the ambiguity of this reversible figure underlines the concept of space as a dynamic presence.

space in which the space between buildings is just as potent as the spaces they contain.

A genealogy of the notion of conceptual space is eloquently documented in Van de Ven's essay entitled *The Theory of Space in Architecture*. In it he pinpoints its birth in the aesthetic theories of the late nineteenth century. It was then that a new awareness of architectonic space as a material entity first became visualized by Art Nouveau designers in their aesthetic amalgamation of ornament and construction. Spurred on by Albert Einstein's initial and general theory of relativity proposed early in the twentieth century, artists and architects became preoccupied with a synthesis of spatial abstraction in the creation of a total work of art - an activity which involved painting, sculpture and, principally, architecture. Initially conceived as an aesthetic and functional concept, the idea of physical space - the most intangible of all means of expression - gradually shifted in favour of functionalism. It became central to the explorations of artists such as Van Doesburg and El Lissitzky and of architects such as Gropius and it proliferated in the teachings of the Bauhaus. In 1953, however, Einstein published his classic and scientific definition of space, an event which was seen to render a variety of spatial interpretations in architecture. In proposing the concept of space as 'place', the concept of absolute space and the relative concept of space-time, his thesis now established three discrete and coherent strands which provide the theoretical base from which any work of architecture develops.

During the twentieth century architectural movements have either intensified the articulation of space or intensified the articulation of form. For example, if the Modern Movement considered space to be its most significant architectural theme, a postmodern aesthetic saw the negative of space, that is, formal mass, surface embellishment and its symbolism, as equally meaningful. More recent theoretical standpoints envisage space and form in equilibrium - an approach expressed in the theory of spatio-plastic unity. Van de Ven describes this theory as finding expression in three ways: exterior space (mass), interior spatial dynamics and their climax in the interpenetration of the two. This culmination of the relationship between interior and urban space returns us to the illusion seen in the vase to face diagram, in which the interface between the two causes both spatial experiences.

Pictorial Space

Our visual experience of space relies upon a hierarchy of optical functions which are triggered by a visual contact with the real world around us. The primary visual signals or cues which aid our perception of depth are binocular vision and motion parallax.

Binocular vision can be divided into three component but related parts: accommodation, convergence and disparity. Accommodation is the ability to focus the eyes on only one point at a time. Convergence is the angle subtended by the two eyes on the object in focus - a nearer object subtending a large angle, a more distant object a smaller angle. Disparity describes the fact that each eye receives a slightly different image from a perceived stimulus. These cues are signalled independently to the brain where they are integrated with all other sensory phenomena to compound a total perception.

Our eyes give overlapping fields of view and stereoscopic depth vision; motion parallax is produced by motions of the head and eyes. Movements at right-angles to a line of vision alter the relative positions of two unequally distant objects, for example, nearer trees and distant hills seen from a moving train will show different relative motion. Motion parallax information can also be perceived by a one-eyed person who, panning like a camcorder, would make extra use of compensatory head movements. Apart from motion pictures and stereoscopic images, all two-dimensional forms of spatial representation equate to the one-eyed

Fig. 33: We can analyse a two dimensional image in many different ways: by linear separation of mass and negative space (A), by identifying the pictorial zones (B), by defining the compositional structure (C), and by delineating its network of constituent shapes (D).

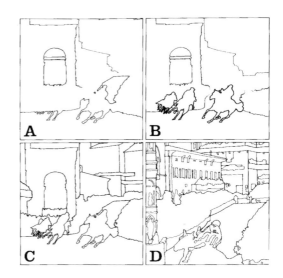

person's view of space but from fixed points - monocular vision lacking the vital head movements and thus precluding the availability of any use of the primary cues to depth.

Impressions on the eye comprise a visual cocktail of signals that are superimposed over a less obvious underlay of structural information. In order to understand how some of these signals work and are transferred into graphic displays, we can 'undress' a visual perception in terms of a drawing to peel away some of its constituent elements. Using the technique of visual analysis, we can isolate the components of a visual experience. This kind of analytical striptease act is useful, not only because it helps us to understand the nature of the seeing process, but also because it aids our understanding of the act of image-building.

Fig 33 (cont.): A complete linear contouring of the image (above) can also be translated as a tonal/colour structure (E, below left), which conveys information about light and surface quality (F, below right).

We can begin our analysis by simply differentiating the figure-ground relationship, the linear separation of the positive (mass) and negative (spatial) areas. To extend this figure-ground analysis, we can now identify the three basic pictorial zones: foreground, middleground and background (fig. 33 A & B). In a further stage of our undressing sequence, we can strip back the image to a line that contours both the number and location of its basic forms (fig. 33 C). This delineated rawness can now be fleshed out using a searching line to describe every discernible shape in the image. If meticulously worked, this analysis discloses a pattern of shapes that combine to form the basic network of the image (fig. 33 D).

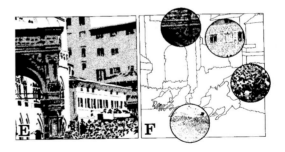

This same linear pattern of perceptual patches can also be translated as a complex network of tonal values that, in either the original scene or its photographic version, reflect colour. Each shape in this network of pattern contains a specific value that, to a greater or lesser degree, differs in tone from that of its neighbours. If we carefully look at the nature of the resulting pattern, we find a fascinating and unpredictable structure of interlocking shapes. A close scrutiny takes us to the very heart of the image, for this is the essential diagram of patches and shapes that is perceived by the eye and translated by the brain into the illusion of space on the two-dimensional plane (fig. 33 E).

The incidence of this pattern of values responds, in turn, to the amount and direction of the light source. We can now isolate this vital ingredient by recording exclusively the precise shapes of only the shades and shadows. If we now turn to the basic delineation of shapes that define the number of formal elements in the original, we find that each presents textural attributes that communicate a range of environmental surfaces. This analysis isolates and identifies a selected number of differently sized planes and shapes that occupy different locations in the illusion of space of the original view. Various types of surface quality are indicated: rough, smooth, glossy, matt, specular, etc. Without such information our original perception would appear a uniformly dull event with little or nothing to be seen (fig. 33 F).

The pictorial images created by graphic displays have, therefore, to rely totally upon the secondary cues to depth: relative apparent size, light and shadow, atmospheric haze and overlap.

Relative Apparent Size (Convergence)

The association of the size of juxtaposed forms with distance is an important depth cue related to a perceptual stance in which more distant objects appear smaller in relation to the viewer's position in space. Although many primitive and traditional representations do not always connotate size fluctuation with depth in pictorial depiction, they do utilize the relative positioning of objects on the picture plane. In Oriental and Asian painting, for instance, objects and figures can, without any size modification, be placed at various heights on the picture plane to convey a strong sense of space.

The position of an object within the frame of a picture is a strong means of assessing spatial location. For instance, the higher an object, the farther back it is assumed to be. We can test this graphic cue by looking down into the space in front of us. What occurs closest to our feet is lower and nearer. As we lift our gaze, objects progressively higher in the field of view appear to us as farther away.

Light and Shadow

The incidence of light, shade and shadow is another vital cue to depth. In a sense, this depth cue is an amalgam of all the others. Our visual image of the real world embodies a complex pattern of perceptual patches; shapes that each have a colour and a tone, and that, apart from responding to the intensity and direction of the light source, each communicate textural attributes describing surface quality which, in turn, describe differently sized planes and shapes that, using different levels of brightness, pinpoint different locations in the illusion of space.

Atmospheric Haze (Aerial Perspective)

This depth cue refers to the perceived greater clarity of nearer points in space in contrast with those more distant. It was Leonardo da Vinci who first discussed this depth-effect in terms of painting when he noticed differences in the quality of colour between points in space; refracting light on dust particles in the atmosphere causing farther objects to appear lighter, more bluish and less clearly defined than objects near at hand.

This phenomenon was first noticed inside a building during the opening of Joseph Paxton's Crystal Palace in 1851. A news report in the *Illustrated London News* describes the experience of Owen Jones' interior colour scheme - comprising reds, yellows and blues on a white background - as follows: 'To appreciate the genius of Owen Jones, one must take his stand at the extremity of the building... Looking up the nave, with its endless rows of pillars the scene vanishes from extreme brightness to the hazy indistinctness which Turner alone could paint'. This reference to 'hazy indistinctness' is the first description of atmospheric haze occurring within a building as in its time the Crystal Palace was the biggest enclosed volume ever constructed (see page 41).

Overlap

The idea that a portion of one object in the field of view is hidden by another instantly informs the eye of a spatial juxtaposition; the hidden area has not ceased to exist, it has simply been removed from view with the implication of a certain distance between the two objects. In other words, our conditioned eye and brain infers a space which has been learned from our visual experience and recreated pictorially by overlap - the partial concealment of further by nearer forms being the most potent of the secondary cues to depth.

The psychologist J.J. Gibson demonstrated the power of this depth cue when he visually tricked subjects in his famous experiment designed to determine the relative importance of the various depth cues. His trick involved cutting away the corner of a larger, nearer playing card precisely where it 'overlapped' the view of a further, smaller playing card when perceived with one eye from a fixed position through a peephole in his viewing apparatus. He found the overlap cue, even when spatially reversed, was so powerful that it negated all other secondary cues to depth (fig. 34).

An important consideration when making pictorial representations which convey illusions of depth is the support on which it is drawn. For example, the very surface texture of drawing paper can countermand the effect of the depth cues by informing the eye that the surface is flat. This accounts for the highly polished finish of *trompe l'oeil* and Super-Realist paintings which to achieve an almost photographic illusion of reality rely upon both

Fig. 34: The cards in Gibson's tests as seen by the subjects, who judged those on the left nearest, and (below) the actual set up, showing that the cards on the right were nearer the subjects.

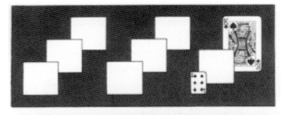

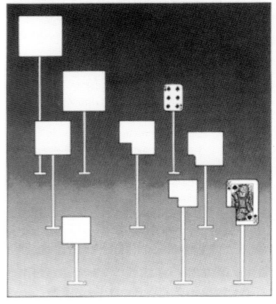

a powerful exploitation of the secondary depth cues and a meticulously flat surface. However, these illusions only occur as long as the pictorial image is beyond the distance where binocular vision is effective and there is no movement away from a fixed point. This can be demonstrated by viewing a painting or a drawing from the side - by moving your viewing position away from the fixed viewpoint any illusion created by the picture is distorted and destroyed.

A further factor must also be accounted for if our representation of space is to be congruent with our perception of reality - the phenomenon of constancy. This is the difference between the image which enters our eye and the image reconstructed by the brain. The phenomenon refers to a zoom-lens capacity of the brain which compensates for the shrinkage of objects with distance. It can be illustrated by the appearance of an audience from a theatre stage; all the faces in the auditorium will look much the same size and yet the retinal image of the nearest faces are larger than those at the back. In viewing photographs or measured perspective drawings, constancy scaling does not readily occur. This is because the camera and the mechanical rules of perspective reproduce the retinal image and not the brain's picture. Artists overcome this problem to some extent by bending the laws of perspective and drawing what they see, that is, at sight size, rather than recreating the retinal image. For example, compare the size of the obelisk in the photograph with that in the same space, the Piazza Navona in Rome, in the painting by Pannini executed in 1756 (figs 35 & 36, and see page 40). The nearer impression of the obelisk seen in the painting results not from the mechanical perspective reflected in the camera's image, but from a perspectival adjustment made in the brain of the artist.

The secondary cues to depth also contribute to our perception of real space but only so far as they can enhance or deny spatial meaning obtained by binocular vision. In qualifying binocular

Figs 35 & 36: The fountain and obelisk in the Piazza Navona, seen in a photograph (left) and in Pannini's painting (right). (See also page 40).

depth information they create illusions and ambiguities which have been pictorially exploited in both a serious and a humorous fashion by such artists as Hogarth, Escher, Albers and Hockney (fig. 37).

In converting two-dimensional messages into three-dimensional meanings, our brain seems to reconstruct space by taking into consideration distance and depth. Space without content, however, is meaningless; space is defined by objects which act as sensory agents - each having perceptual properties of their own such as size, shape, surface and form. To extend our dialogue with experience, we now turn to a consideration of these elements.

Fig. 37: One consistent perspective system is used to create a fusion of different spatial worlds: M.C. Escher *High and Low,* **copyright 1997, Cordon Art, Barn, Holland. All rights reserved.**

The Spatial Elements

'Variety is not just the spice of life, it is the very stuff of it.'

J. Vernon

The Spatial Elements

Part of our legacy from the Renaissance is a notion of form and
volume as defined by the visual elements - line, shape, colour
texture and form. Most present-day design courses are founded
on this principle, whose fundamentals were re-expounded afresh
in the Bauhaus by teachers including Johannes Itten, Paul Klee
and Wassily Kandinsky. Their educational philosophy, examining
the spatial experience and coordination of design from fundamentals, has contributed a great deal to the designers'
understanding of the potential of formal arrangement. However,
a fragmentation in spatial analysis, however unavoidable, can lead
to a schismatic approach to environmental design, an attitude
which isolates consideration of the interaction of form and void
from its interface - the surface elements.

By comparison our real perception of space is subject to a holistic
process, an integrated faculty in which each spatial variable is experienced in context with all the others, as in a kaleidoscope. To
take one example, our perception of colour is constantly and simultaneously modified by a supplementary experience of light,
texture and form; in other words, colour is light, texture and
form. We experience each of the spatial elements as a component of all the others. But a glimpse over the architect's shoulder
finds his or her initial visualization of space traditionally born in
the convention of line, and drawings have come to exist as a kind
of instantly recognizable 'signature' of their authors. Compare, for
instance, the calligraphic dash of an emotionally-charged Erich
Mendelsohn sketch with brittle incisions of an Antonio Sant'Elia perspective with the technical precision of Vladimir Tatlin's elevation
(figs 38, 39 & 40).

Line and Rhythm
Architecture is not experienced in lines, but their characteristics
can reflect in microcosm the expression of various architectural
philosophies. The line also signifies a rhythmic, directional energy; a scale of emotional ups and downs equating to their rise

and fall. Upward curves elicit a sense of cheerfulness while their descending counterparts register a corresponding emotional slump. When the stability of straight lines loses control, its zig-zag pulsation assumes such an emotional electricity that it has attracted both the attentions of psychologists and more scientific artists.

A zig-zag linear decoration was highly popular in primitive cultures and, on tracing its journey through architectural time and space its pulsating rhythm - after this primitive cavorting - was harnessed to a structure of harmonic, gilded proportion upon which to hang the flesh of ancient concepts of space. The Gothic builder ordered the line to skyrocket, then the Renaissance commanded it to chase Brunelleschi's vanishing dot through horizontal layers of ordered space and into infinity. After its adolescence - scribbling its way around the delights of Baroque confectionery - its rhythmic pulse began a gradual descent into a premature senility, occasionally flickering with excitement in the minds of more creative designers. Until exposed by modern painters, a linear scaffolding had lurked between canvas and paint, whose ambiguities Albers examined and which escaped from the confines of the picture plane and spread, via De Stijl and Constructivist drawing-boards, into the built environment.

Set against some spectacular performances in the stimulation-seeking eyes of artists the line was to become bent on right-angles, seemingly responding to Mondrian's vision of a spatial world in complete submission to the grid. More recently, however, the line has been commissioned to revisit and re-explore the rhythms of classical form, to question and disrupt perspectival order and to underwrite a conceptual architecture derived from theories of language and its multiple meanings. But, in generating rhythm, line is simply a two-dimensional construct of reality, merely an illusion.

Figs 38,39 & 40: Drawings by Erich Mendelsohn (for the Einstein Tower, top), by Vladimir Tatlin (for the Monument ot the Third International project in Moscow, facing) and by Antonio Sant'Elia (for the Città Nuova project, above).

Colour

As part of their characteristics, however, the architectural elements have surface quality. As such, they are governed by the same laws that apply to the other spatial elements but, unfortunately, surface colour and texture seem to occur in our built environment more by accident or whim than by design. For this reason we should first understand why and how it is we are fortunate enough to be endowed with the faculty of colour vision.

Look carefully at the colour wheel on page 68. Focus on the white dot at its centre and allow the surrounding colours to be completely absorbed by the eye. After about a minute or so focusing intently at this figure, switch your gaze to the black dot below.

You should now experience an illusion of the colour wheel. If you did, you experienced a 'negative afterimage' in which you saw colour where none existed. This demonstration is important because it clearly illustrates that the ultimate colour experience occurs not in the eye but in the brain. In other words, the colours that we see do not exist on the surface of objects but are 'manufactured' in the mind's eye. Our experience of colour is a subjective sensation conveyed by the eye's absorption of the different energies in different wavelengths of light radiation within the visible spectrum. However, without an observer, light rays do not, in themselves, constitute colour.

As Sir Isaac Newton explained in his *Optiks*, 'The rays are not coloured. In them there is nothing else than a power to stir up a sensation of this or that colour'. The eye and brain of the observer interprets the meaning of these sensory messages; the resultant colour perception depends on three important factors. First, the conditions under which the stimulus is viewed: for example, certain paint colours applied under tungsten light would appear very different from the same colours viewed in sunlight, as the two perceptions respond to two different spectral energy

distributions contained in each light source. Second, a colour perception depends on the spectral characteristics of the stimulus,
the ability of its substance to absorb, reflect or transmit light: red
paint, for instance, appears as red because it has the property of
absorbing from white light everything except the red component
of the light. The third factor is our ability to perceive colours, the
sensitivity of our colour-registering mechanism (the eye and brain)
to create a colour response.

In reaching the eyes, sensory messages of wavelength are decoded by light-sensitive nerve cells located in the retina and
known as rods which give a perception of white, grey and black.
Also located in the retina are around 50,000 colour receptors
known as cones. In a colour response they are fired by light
wavelengths of red, green and blue, and convey messages along
the optic nerve for their ultimate experience in the visual projection region of the brain. The idea that colour is seen in the brain
is, therefore, correct in this sense for we can experience colour
with our eyes shut as in dreams. The existence of our personal
Technicolor processing laboratory is further exampled in the incidence of anomalous colour vision, popularly miscalled colour
blindness, due to one or more sets of cones either misfiring or
being completely out of action.

The question 'What causes the afterimage?' is still an open one.
Nobody really knows, but the best theory is offered by Ewald
Hering's Theory of Opponent Colour, proposed in 1872. He argued that the explanation lies in the fact that the colour
receptors in the eye (cones) are grouped in pairs. For instance,
when you looked at the red sector of the colour wheel, the receptor that was 'fired' by the red stimulus switched off and
caused the involuntary 'firing' of its neighbour, green. So, when
you saw the afterimage, you may have noticed that the colours
in the illusion were not in the same place. They appeared as

complementary colours, or those 'opposite' the colours seen in the original image.

If the question 'How do we see colour?' is still an open one, then the question 'Why do we see colour?' is also open to interpretation. The best answer is found in the work of zoologists who suggest that our evolution of colour vision is intimately linked to the evolution of colour on the surface of our planet. In a world without colour what use would colour vision be? Even before colour vision evolved, some living tissues were already coloured - blood was 'red' and foliage 'green'. However, the most striking colours of nature, those found in flowers, birds and fish were all evolutionary creations deliberately developed to act as visual signals, carrying messages to those eyes equipped to perceive them. This theory also speculates that the early tree-dwelling primates later moved in on an ecological niche previously occupied by birds who could already see colour. In order to survive, to compete effectively with birds, primates needed to evolve colour vision. Consequently, according to the Land Theory, the clustering of red and green cones in the retina evolved first, possibly directly responding to the need to spot ripened red berries and fruits against foliage in the hunt for food. However, the later emergence of humankind developed this part of the evolutionary survival kit into a new skill - the ability to apply colour where it does not naturally occur.

Colour and Form

After its genesis in the painted Neolithic caves, the history of architectural colour and form continued through the gilding and colour-washing of ancient Greek temples and the medieval cathedrals. Later seen as appealing directly to the senses, such decoration came to be suppressed by successive waves of ethical and formal cleansing. First it vanished under a seventeenth century Puritanical whitewash and early this century it was again banished by orthodox Modernists who saw colour as bypassing the prescribed filter of reason. During the last three decades, however, architectural colour has slowly made a comeback to the drawing-boards of some architects to resume its role, albeit often a subjective one, as a potent facet of the language of form.

An important historical event in the relationship between colour and its perception took place in the mid-nineteenth century when Owen Jones devised his scientific coloration for Paxton's Crystal Palace. Based on a developing interest in the theory of colour vision, Jones' scheme for the columns and superstructure followed Eugene Chevreul's rules for colour clarity and George Field's law of proportion. This proportional harmonic related three parts yellow to five parts red to eight parts blue against a field of white. Seen close at hand Jones' colours were legible to the eye but over distance an optical mixing took place, causing the forms to progressively diffuse into a blue-grey haze (see page 41). This erosion of form was again the subject of experiment in the early part of the twentieth century when De Stijl designers such as Theo van Doesburg and Gerrit Rietveld used primary hues visually to disrupt, dissolve and displace architectural planes. Their methodology employed the apparent spatial effects of advancing and receding hues to dramatically modify a perception of cubic volumes.

A study of how architects use colour today shows the extension of two basic traditions. First, there is its symbolic use - a function that spans from the colours of the Parthenon to its representational use by architects like John Outram and Michael Graves. Graves suggests that no matter how one might know colour to be an application to a surface, we see colour first as an expression of form. In other words, if a concrete wall is coloured terra cotta in order to allude to brick, the first perceptual reaction to that surface is of brick. Outram has described his use of colour and pattern as a medium to dematerialize a solid and orderly architecture; to use colour as an *aide mémoire* to link the extreme past to a view of the future. In the hands of such architects, together with those such as Libeskind, Eisenman and Tschumi who use colour as a powerful component of a Deconstructivist language, this symbolic colour use represents one aspect of an architectural tradition that has occupied designers throughout the history of building: the deliberate and symbolic placement of a man-made object in the landscape.

A second tradition concerns the careful integration of a built form that is more akin to the earth, either constructed from the same materials on which it stands or colour-blended into the surrounding setting. The first approach is aggressive, the second passive; compare, for example, a Le Corbusier white house or a Richard Meier museum in a green field with a Frank Lloyd Wright house of the same colour as the earth, or in ancient times humankind living in a cave at the same time as they built temples (see illustrations on pages 72 and 73).

The Colour Dimensions

Several attempts have been made to design a world of colour notation, but all can be traced back to the work of Sir Isaac Newton who, in 1660, recreated a spectrum by directing a narrow beam of white light through a prism. Newton then conceptually formed his spectrum into a colour wheel by taking its two ends and bending it into a circle. He had created the first colour circle and had invented a convenient format for the first of the three attributes or dimensions of colour - hue (fig. 41). Hue is that quality which is commonly accepted as colour in defining its redness, blueness and yellowness.

If we mentally visualize the colour circle as occupying a horizontal plane and then pierce its centre with a grey, vertical axis we complete the basic coordinates of the colour-space. Descending in a stepped scale of grey from white at the top to black at the bottom, this achromatic scale represents the second of the colour dimensions - blackness (value).

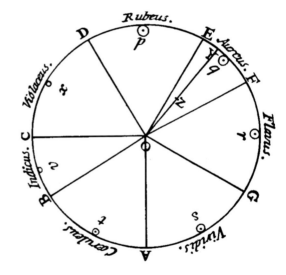

Fig. 41: Isaac Newton's colour circle.

The third colour dimension is chromaticness (chroma), i.e., a conceptualized horizontal scale of diminishing colour strength as the bright and unsullied hues on the equator of the circle become progressively muted and desaturated as they step back toward the central achromatic scale.

As each colour perception - if not of a pure hue - will embody a degree of relationship between the three dimensions, it becomes possible to calibrate in three-dimensional colour-space all the nuances in the visible colour realm. Indeed, the basis of this model has, over the years, led to various colour systems each enlisting a different geometrical model in their claim to provide an exhaustive and accurate means of colour identification (fig. 42).

Colour Psychology

Psycho-physiological research has found that reactions to colour through the eye (and skin) are many, varied and intriguing. For example, the researcher Kurt Goldstein wrote: 'It is probably not a false statement if we say that a specific colour stimulation is accompanied by a specific response pattern in the entire organism'. Summarizing his work, he suggests that the perception of colour affects muscular tension, brain waves, heart rate, respiration and other functions of the autonomic nervous system, and certainly it arouses definite emotional and aesthetic responses.

However, the speculation and myth surrounding the meanings we associate with colour paints a confusing picture. Yellow, for instance, has been suggested as a good colour for libraries and classrooms as it was thought to stimulate the intellect, but art therapists have observed that suicidally inclined patients tend to use yellow pigment generously in their painting - as, indeed, did Van Gogh. Red is seen stereotypically as a powerful, active colour while green, on the other hand, has traditionally been thought of as calming. On this basis it has been used for both prison cells and hospitals, in an attempt to pacify involuntary guests. Blue is

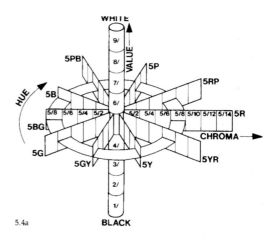

Fig. 42: The three-dimensional world of colour as devised by Albert Munsell in 1915.

seen as a cool, lightweight and recessive colour and is less clearly focused on the eye than the so-called warmer and heavier red-based hues. This spatial effect was first noted by Leonardo da Vinci and subsequent generations of painters who have understood that different areas of coloured paint can occupy different positions in space.

More recent research conducted in Sweden challenges some of the common attributes we associate with colours. In contrast to the earlier laboratory-confined work, the Swedish studies measured colour judgements against real architecture or in mock-ups of life-sized architectural settings. The importance of the three colour dimensions of hue, chromaticness and blackness are central to these findings. Their exhaustive investigations question, for example, the common idea that green colours have a calming effect. They found that people do not consider a red to be more active or stimulating than a green or, indeed, any other hue - so long as the colours viewed are of equal chromaticness and blackness. In all the tests they discovered that the dimensions of hue, i.e., the greenness, redness, or yellowness of colour, was much less important in environmental colour than chromaticness or blackness. For example, all dark colours were seen as being more masculine, more unusual and heavier than light colours and that the former tend to reduce space and define it less clearly when judged in comparison with their tinted counterparts. Lighter colours, on the other hand, were judged as being more friendly, more cultured and more pleasant, and also rated as appearing more beautiful than the darker colours.

In the context of colour temperature, the Swedish studies support the traditional belief that red appears warm and blue cold, except that a blue-red was judged as being as visually cool as the blues and blue-greens. However, one Swedish researcher, Lars Sivik, underlines the importance of contextual reference and the interaction of colour and surface texture. Consider the following question: 'Which of the two appear warmer - an ice-blue woollen sock or a red plastic bag?'.

Light and Colour

Light is the medium through which we see colour. Sunlight is another dynamic that profoundly affects our impression of colour because as the sun moves across the sky the quality of its light will change with every moment of the day. Generally speaking, early morning light is yellowish becoming bluish at midday before tending to redden at dusk. Therefore, as buildings are seen at all times of the day, sunlight is constantly changing the impression of their colour. Not only changing in day and seasonal cycles, light quality can vary in space. For instance, a particular blue seen under sunlight in Greece will appear quite different from the same blue viewed under sunlight in Britain. Furthermore, different types of electric light will cause the same hue to appear differently (see page 69).

We can attune to minor colour shifts using a visual and mental process called 'colour constancy'. This aspect of our colour vision allows the familiar colours of objects to retain their 'normal' colour appearance despite changes in the colour of the light source. But there are occasions when colours which seem correct in one setting appear 'wrong' when viewed in another. This is emphasized in photographs taken under fluorescent light which, when compared with those taken in sunlight, appear colour distorted. Similarly, a comparison of different types of electric lighting reveals a wide variation in colour rendering. For example, a red viewed under tungsten light appears orange while the same red under white fluorescent tubes looks bluish. When red is seen in the yellowish sodium of street lamps it appears as a brown and when viewed in the greenish light from mercury lamps it appears almost black.

Whether applied, or integral with the material of its fabric, the colour of architecture functions as a modulator of the colour-rendering

properties of light. In other words, as sunlight, with its visible spectrum complete with its mixture of wavelengths, falls across the surfaces of a building, it becomes modified - to be reflected, scattered or absorbed in the final colour perception. But, apart from the psycho-physiological effects, there is another dimension to this perception of surface which is also optically illuminated - that of texture.

Texture

Texture and colour play an important role in the environment at large for, in their modulation of surface, they signal scale and depth. They can also define zones of territorial space by communicating go and no-go areas. For example, in Oxford's medieval backstreets variegated surface treatments not only demarcate individual facades but also the transitional zones between 'public' and 'private' such as the smooth stone paving that connects walkways to front doors and the areas of cobblestones that keep prying eyes away from front windows (figs 43 & 44). Similarly, in the islands of the Cyclades in Greece the annual ritual of colour-washing villages houses and pavements reflects a redefinition of the close working relationship of interpersonal space - the progressive buildup of decorative pigment softening the corners of forms and 'welding' vertical to horizontal.

Just as there are three dimensions of colour, the psychologist Sven Hesselgren has outlined three dimensions of touch. The first is the actual sensation of physical contact with the surface of an object, such as moving the finger or the hand backwards and forwards at the point of contact. Hesselgren cites the studies of E.H. Webber who demonstrated that if the hand or fingertips did not move it was difficult to distinguish between one texture and another. The second dimension can be expressed as we pick up an object - such as an ink bottle. In holding the object we gain an immediate impression of its weight - this tactile sensation being recorded by the kinaesthetic activity of our muscles which make

Figs 43 & 44: Floorscape textures in Oxford (above) signal semi-private and public domains (Photo courtesy Mike Jenks). Lime-washed walls and floorscape in a Greek island village (below).

infinitesimal adjustments to the balance of our body in space. If we now close our eyes and, using the hands, explore the entire surface of the object, we experience a third dimension of touch - a haptic perception of its form. This sensation is the most reliable of our sense organs in acquiring knowledge of the existence of a physical form - feeling is believing!

The thrill of touch can span scales of roughness and smoothness and temperature ranges from the warmth of polystyrene to the chill of steel. There are scales of plasticity ranging from hard and inert to elastic, tactile sensations that can also be accompanied by experiences of pleasure and pain. The thrill of touch at architectural scale is exemplified by those who cross the lawn fronting I.M. Pei's National Gallery in Washington DC to stroke the pointed edge of his acutely wedge-shaped building; the result of these countless caresses not only disfiguring the immaculate lawn but leaving a permanent grease mark on the wall. Mysteriously drawn to this tactile ritual, visitors seem to feel the need to reaffirm some visual disbelief or to take part in some symbolic ceremony. It is an intensely physical act which ranks with the good-luck ritual of kissing the Blarney Stone or the religious devotion of kissing the toe of Michelangelo's Pieta in St Peter's in Rome.

However, architecture is not experienced exclusively by our fingertips and our feet, but by the whole of our bodies. For instance, the ergonomic architecture of the chair takes us through a wide range of bodily sensation (fig. 45). Compare the hard, ungiving wooden planes of Rietveld's Red-Blue-Yellow Chair against the elasticated membrane of Archizoom's triangulation. Again, compare the kinaesthetic feel of the swivelling luxury of the Eames leather-lined barber chair with the suspension of the common but ingenious deck-chair, or the bounce of an inflatable armchair with the icy austerity of Plia's plexiglass and the rigid formality of a church pew. Such sensory excursions into diversity should not be confined to a second-hand experience - such as reading - but

Fig. 45: The various tactile attributes of 'body architecture' shown in a range of chairs.

Fig. 46: A colour wheel (facing): see page 58.
Fix your eye on the centre of the colour circle for a few
minutes and then move your gaze to look at the black dot
below the circle. You should experience the illusion of a
negative after image - proof that the colour experience is in
the brain.

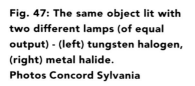

Fig. 47: The same object lit with
two different lamps (of equal
output) - (left) tungsten halogen,
(right) metal halide.
Photos Concord Sylvania

reading - but gained from direct contact; the nature of tactile perception being heightened by the thrill of contrasting physical contact with form.

Meanwhile, mainstream architecture continues to overindulge in the polish of a machine aesthetic - smoothness and blandness not always resulting from cheaply and mass-produced materials. A predilection for bland, smooth surface is epitomized in a Meisian gloss which erased the embossed words 'Bethlehem Steel' from the metal framework of his Farnsworth glass house. This is a far cry from the surface delights of Gaudí's scintillating porcelain mosaics (see page 36), the feathery shingles of Herb Greene's 'prairie chicken' (see page 74) and from the rich stone texture of Dimitri Pikionis' urban 'carpet' (figs. 48 & 49).

The 'carpet' is the paved footpath installed under the supervision of the late Dimitri Pikionis on the southwestern approaches of the Acropolis in Athens between 1954-57. It exists not only as an act of devotion by an architect who expressed extreme sensitivity and skill in creating a humble footpath, but it also demonstrates a sublime working relationship between the texture perceived by the eye and the tactile sensation detected underfoot.

Designed to meet the increased needs of modern tourism, Pikionis' aim was to create a stone landscape which allowed visitors pedestrian access to the Acropolis while avoiding any dramatic imposition on the site or its history. Consequently, complete with its stepped sequence of viewing-points and integrated clusters of seating and pavilions, the plan of the pathway sensitively reflects the topology of its setting by simply following the ancient pathways that had naturally been imprinted on the hill over countless centuries of use. The paving comprises limestone blocks and marble offcuts found in the disused Athenian quarries. Sometimes hewn into shape, sometimes broken, the slabs are laid and separated by distinctive joints which,

Figs 48 & 49: Two views of Dimitri Pikionis's paved footpath on the south-western approaches to the Acropolis in Athens

incorporating small differences in their widths together with the occasional insertion of linear marble 'anchoring rods', transform the walking surface into a mesmerizing mosaic of large and small geometrical shapes. This incredible pattern of paving did not result from the drawing-board nor from any extensive pre-planning. Rather, it stemmed from the creative and on-site improvisation of Pikionis, a small group of his design students and a team of masons. What is so beautiful about this project is that it took its final form from the undulation encountered along its route - construction responding directly to the human eye, the immediate nature of the terrain and the quality of light.

Once laid, the surface of the stone was worked over with hammer, chisel and crowbar to record the 'vital pulse' of the texture on its surface - a process that not only increased friction but caused tiny indentations to catch sunlight and thereby highlight a secondary layer of textural grain. To increase the variegation during this treatment, Pikionis would always encourage the masons to accentuate rather than regulate minor differences.

Although completed almost four decades ago, Pikionis' achievement in this comparatively modest project still stands as one of the most superb examples of surface treatment. In insisting on the significance of 'place' as the basis of artistic creation, and attempting to connect the installation with both the site and to a collective vernacular memory, he elevates the humble footpath to the status of a horizontal work of art.

Scale

As well as its role as a tactile modulator of form and its surface, an optical reading of texture signals depth and scale. On the one hand, it is the diminishing gradients of textural pattern which intensify linear perspective - an effect which psychologists such as J.J. Gibson find such an important facet of our spatial under-

Figs 50 & 51: Richard Meier's High Museum of
Art, Atlanta, photographed by Richard Bryant/
Arcaid, (facing) and Frank Lloyd Wright's
Falling Water, Bear Run, Pennsylvania (below,
courtesy Sandak Inc.) illustrate respectively a
synthetic, aggressive colour strategy and one
that is organic and passive.

standing. On the other hand, textures communicate a sense of scale. For example, the pattern of jointwork in Pikionis' pathway together with those in all horizontal and vertical planes regulate a sense of scale against which we judge our own size. To tamper with this human scale relationship, for example by introducing oversized units or elements, is to both disrupt the scalar grain of the built environment as well as unsettle its user.

Much architectural design is visualized at a scale allowed only by the confines of the drawing-board. Therefore, the bigger the formal concept, the smaller its size on the board and the farther away the designer's mind's eye from the complexity of the idea. Masterly architects such as Carlo Scarpa have successfully bridged this gap using a zoom-lens attention to detail. By focusing down to a fine-tuned articulation of minutiae at the point of contact between user and building, this approach brings delight to an architectural experience at close proximity.

The sculptor Claes Oldenburg has played imaginative games with architectural scale. Much of his inventive reversal of scale involves siting colossal versions of everyday objects in popular city spaces - some, such as the giant clothes-peg in Philadelphia, being realized through his sculpture. His London projects proposed the installation of an enormous ball-cock on the Thames, replaced Nelson's Column with a car rear-view mirror and removed Eros from Piccadilly Circus to make way for a massive lipstick. The humour of his vision of American architectural form has dreamed-up binocular buildings in collaboration with Frank O. Gehry, hypodermic skyscrapers, and a giant ice-lolly as a street junction (fig. 53). There are also examples in today's architecture of this Gulliverian effect. For example, Vladimir Tatlin's leaning Helter-Skelter project (see page 56), Jørn Utzon's sails, Skidmore, Owings and Merrills' concrete doughnut (figs. 57 & 58, pages 78 & 79) and Philip Johnson's Lipstick Building . Such architecture can take on a little warmth and humour but also counterpoint the

Fig. 52: Roof detail on Herb Greene's Oklahoma 'prairie chicken' house.

fact that such human responses are not always intended within
the icy strictures of a rationalist philosophy.

Pyramids of Need; Ladders of Taste

In designing for the built milieu the architect, rather like an organ-
ist, can manipulate the scales and rhythms of a spatial keyboard;
through pulling and depressing the design stops the architect can
also control the volume and variety of its variables. The orchestration of a built environment created by many apparently
tone-deaf architects makes for a pervading monotony which bor-
rows little from any real articulation of the spatial elements. The
early sensory deprivation experiments conducted in the 1950s
demonstrate that withdrawal of stimulation can be just as injuri-
ous to the human organism as the opposite effects of overkill.

In proposing a theory to account for deprivation J.A. Vernon
states: 'The human cannot long endure a homogeneous situation
no matter how good and desirable it is.' Another researcher, E.
Miller, said that the brain needs constantly varying forms of
stimulation in order to operate. As a result of this and later work,
we begin to understand that the human organism and its nervous
system actually seek a contrasting sensory stimulation which is
rarely provided for in mainstream architecture. In much modern
architecture the seemingly endless search for uniformity appears
to fly in the face of our search for experiential diversity. For example, consider the quest for uniformity in lighting levels and the
equalization of room temperature compared with the experience
of moving between intense and gloomy illumination or the passage from cool to warm pockets of air. Together with the
blandness of surface elaboration, this unvarying approach - possibly under the philosophical cloak of unity - seems diametrically
opposed to all that is important to our spatial experience.

In order to understand more fully this sterility, we have to consider two differing perceptions of that shrine to architectural

**Fig. 53: Claes Oldenburg project
for a giant ice-lolly as a street
barrier. Courtesy Claes Oldenburg**

colour

Figs 54 (facing), 55 & 56 (below): The opulent interior of the Madonna Inn (see page 83), compared to a reconstruction of the colours of the Parthenon (in Alma-Tadema's *Pheidias Painting the Frieze of the Parthenon*, courtesy Birmingham Museums & Art Gallery) and the visual extravaganza of the fairground.

perfection - the Parthenon. Seen through rationalist eyes, it epitomizes a zenith in spatial-formal purity, and functions as a study source in monochromatic excellence. However, through the eyes of its designers, Ictinus and Callicrates, it was completely colourwashed, painted and gilded - its decorative elements detailed in primary hues. They would have been puzzled by its modern interpretation for, on its opening day in 432 BC, they had intended its rich and colourful appearance to represent their concept of purity, for its Greek name implies 'virginity' (fig. 55, page 77). Through an informed archaeologist's eye, an ancient Greek city would equate to the exuberance and vulgarity commonly associated with the sensory excitation of a fairground. This is because an ancient conception of urban design was that of a total work of art whose spaces breathed texture, colour and form; rich in sensory experience they were created by multi-disciplined designers who envisaged achievements as a synthesis of painting, sculpture and architecture.

To explain the modern designer's misconception of the Parthenon, one has to return to the separation of the roles of the artist and the architect at the birth of specialism in the Italian Renaissance. This bifurcation was caused when a new process of making an art-for-its-own-sake was encouraged by a wealthy patronage. Since then, fine art and architecture have pursued separate paths with little interaction - dichotomy depriving the environmental designer of any real expertise in the multi-sensory handling of space. Meanwhile, the sculptor examines the diversity of interplay between solid form, tactile sensation and the empty space surrounding it, while the painter privately investigates colour-form relationships in the uninhabitable world of two dimensions. The lines of demarcation between artists and architects are further exemplified in the continuing debate concerning the integration of art into the built environment. This debate rarely addresses the concept of an integrated 'artistic' architecture but, instead, focuses on the insertion of art objects either in, on or near public

Figs 57 & 58: Jørn Utzon's 'sails' for the Sydney Opera House (above, photo Harry Sowden) and the Hirshhorn Gallery in Washington DC, by Skidmore Owings & Merrill (facing).

buildings. Few artists or architects work at this interface, a situation which, when a piece of art is installed in a public place, attracts the familiar and disparaging 'turd in the piazza' criticism. Obviously, the architect can learn much from the artist through, for instance, participation in multi-disciplinary design projects or a serious engagement in the percentage for art initiatives, but the architect can also gain much from a simple study of the predilections of ordinary people.

For instance, a test conducted by the author and psychologist Byron Mikellides investigated comparative responses to degrees of colour on buildings between architects and laypeople. Throughout the test - involving the rating of various images of brightly coloured buildings - laypeople consistently recorded their preference for more colour than the taste of our architectural subjects would allow. Throughout the test, the lay subjects constantly associated more bland and monochrome architectural examples in their minds with 'bunkers' and 'prisons'; responses which are so common they have become a cliché.

Similarly, as part of his redefinition of 'defensible space' (as part of an upgrading programme for a lowbrow housing project in New York City), Oscar Newman discovered a highly favourable response amongst his resident clients when he intensified their environmental degrees of texture, colour and space. In explaining this response, Newman cites the sociologist, Lee Rainwater, who has projected the idea of a social ladder of taste in which each rung of society aspires to the one above.

According to Rainwater, the architect sits at the top of the ladder and functions as taste-maker, with only the rich and sophisticated possessing the capacity to enjoy the severity of the harsh existence he or she tends to advocate. The majority at the bottom aspire to the middle-class stratum, and to their basic drive for shelter is added a desire for cosiness and variety with higher degrees of colour, texture and appearance. Such a need is also illustrated in the enormous growth of the do-it-yourself industry which brings the lay person into personal involvement with the building process. In this context, Rainwater's projection can be directly linked to Maslow's 'pyramid of needs' in which a person's basic need for protection from the elements and an everyday interaction with a building - opening and closing windows and doors, touching handrails and taps - is superseded by an even more active and profound experience. This higher level of participation in our surroundings - expressed in styrofoam covings, elaborate wallpapers, fitted pine kitchens and conservatories - represents a deep need for self-fulfilment.

This basic drive for cosiness is also encountered in a test which demonstrated that beneath a superficial layer of good taste - even in the upper class - there lurks a healthy thirst for a decorative diversity. This test monitored the use of two waiting rooms: one austere and filled with chrome and leather furniture against white walls, the other 'jazzy' and decorated in heavy colours, chintzy fabrics and kitsch furnishings. During the test, questionnaires and interviews conducted outside the rooms elicited a favourable response to the 'Swedish' style room, but a more discrete surveillance found that the vast majority had actually waited in the 'vulgar' room.

Among the psychological studies which suggest that people have little impact on their urban setting, the work of Peter Smith is worth noting. He has made a synoptic study of the primitive or limbic brain - that undernourished portion in the right hemisphere of our grey matter which apparently is deprived of all that sensory stimulation upon which it thrives: richness, ornateness, sparkle and colour. Smith proposes that we have, for psychophysiological stimulation, to escape into spaces in which the volume of its perception is amplified, as it finds little satisfaction

Fig. 59: Active vernacular: self-built seaside chalets at Jaywick Sands. Photo Mike Jenks

in the dull environments created by the brain's dominant and intellectual left hemisphere.

Whenever an environment ceases to excite, we find that its inhabitants, when given the option, tend to vote with their feet. In order to discover their alternatives we should as designers observe the kinds of place to which they are attracted. For, in doing so, we discover environments rich in spatial diversity - a glorious, popular architecture of bad taste.

We find this spatial diversification in pleasure environments: theme parks, World Fairs, Coney Islands and Golden Miles; we can discover it along the American strip where motels and diners take on forms reminiscent of the work of Claes Oldenburg. Along coastlines there is a wealth of celebratory and thematic architecture responding to the ocean: ship-shaped inns, the variegated cabins of Jaywick Sands, Seaside, Port Grimaud, together with a Scottish boat-shaped castle where the original owner (a seasick Admiral) could survey his fleet from its walls. Inland we can find splendid examples of an architectural dissimilitude: grottoes, follies, and the superb fantasies of Edward James in Mexico and of Clough Williams-Ellis in Wales. Most of this alternative architecture compels a response, even if it is only a smile or a raised eyebrow (figs. 59, 60 & 61).

The Search for Diversity

As part of our education in 'bad taste', let us observe the way in which people modify their environments. The need to personalize and territorialize, especially in monotonous settings, finds a synaesthetic use of paint to either intensify the organic colour of brickwork or, indeed, to transform magically its appearance into that of stone. There is the vertical crazy-paving of sham stone cladding - used as much to decorate as to insulate. There is also the heightening of textural pattern in the use of complementary hues for bricks and for mortar joints - the search for personaliza-

Figs 60 & 61: Architectural indulgence: Port Meirion, Wales, by Clough Williams-Ellis (above). The site gained cult status as the setting for the 1960s TV drama *The Prisoner*. (Below) Holiday homes in Port Grimaud, a modern Mediterranean village.

tion and territorialization even extending to the 'bicoloured downspout' on which each side of boundary drainpipes is meticulously painted in the respective and emblematic colours of joint ownership. Such a study will find a wealth of spatial articulation expressed in multicoloured and texturally variegated paving, fantastic topiary, dream-fulfilling wishing-wells, stick-on Georgian plastic porches and, of course, the ubiquitous garden gnome (fig. 62).

Such modification, elaboration and decoration seems to function as a crucial aspect of the experience of built form; it seems to elevate the concept of 'house' to that of 'home'. Moreover, this decorative approach embodies a rich and symbolic dimension - possibly the most potent being the symbol of hope expressed in the sunrise emblem found in leaded-windows, doors, fences and gates. This symbolic association of architectural elements with aspects of our future and past is an important aspect of our understanding of architecture. There is the Classical detailing which carried over from the earliest wooden structures into the marble of Greek temples - an architectural genealogy that resurfaced briefly in the banalities of postmodernism. Religious architecture is filled with the symbolism of number and orientational significance: the twelve bays of a chapel denoting the twelve apostles, the trefoil window signifying the Holy Trinity and the east-facing facade pointing to the birthplace of Christ, etc. However, in taking such loving care about the orchestration of colour, texture and form in, on and around their homes, the ordinary person is a designer being guided, not by profound theology or philosophy, but by a basic human instinct for a sense of place.

To conclude our quest for diversity in built form, here are two examples of a total integration of spatial variables in quite different monuments to the non-designer. The first is a motel known as the Madonna Inn. Built alongside Route 101 near San Luis Obispo in

Fig. 62: A topiary model of HMS Verity, created in his garden at Hanborough, Oxfordshire, by Arthur Leach, former leading seaman on the vessel. Photo Iradj Parvaneh

California, the Inn is an extraordinary work of architecture, designed and built as a labour of love by a family of non-architects. The Inn sits on a hill not far from William Randolph Hearst's celebrated castle but, whereas Hearst's opulent San Simeon is a monument to wealth and power, the Inn is a monument to a vivid imagination (figs 63 & 64, and see page 76).

Its sprawling complex contains 110 rooms each conceived around a different theme to provide an environment of pure fantasy - a kind of Disneyland for adults. Built with neither architectural training nor blueprint, the Inn is filled with sumptuous and distinctive interiors. Several of its bedrooms are circular with names like 'Cloud Nine' and 'Vienna Suite'. Some are completely lined with enormous boulders - collected by the landlord during his earlier role as a road-builder. Bathrooms are grottoes complete with rock fixtures and large circular rock-lined showers from which water 'rains' from the ceiling. The Inn is especially renowned for its waterfall urinals: step up to them, step back and - swoosh - the huge waterfall washes all away. Relieved only by the occasional blue or green, the Inn is colour-schemed throughout in a hot, bubble-gum pink. There are pink telephones, signs, lamp posts and gas station pumps - even the bread baked in the pink bakery is dyed in the same hue. Garish by some standards, glamorous by others, the widespread use of fountains, stained-glass windows, cupid chandeliers, canopy beds and crystal bath fittings, completes the glitz and the glitter, Although some critics may sneer at the apparent kitsch, the Inn has featured in architectural journals and its rooms are fully-booked months in advance. Indeed, the late Charles Moore described Madonna Inn as 'one of the most surprising (and surprisingly full) experiences to be found'. It is the remarkable success of such an environment that begs the question as to its enormous appeal. The Inn seems to satisfy some Alice in Wonderland need for fantasy, humour and glamour. In other words, it appears to be attractive to that part of the

Figs 63 & 64: Two interiors at the Madonna Inn: a bedroom (above), and the waterfall urinal (below).

brain that has been denied by the quality of the mainstream built environment.

The second example stands in a nondescript sector of Los Angeles and was built by an Italian immigrant, Simon Rodia. His towers at Watts have signified many things for many people but, above all, they represent a synthesis between the Renaissance-formed categories of painting (colour), sculpture (surface and form) and architecture (human space) in a single environmental statement. This do-it-yourself structure is also remarkable in that its humble creator constructed it directly into space without the aid of scaffolding and machinery and, more interestingly, entirely without any preparatory designs on paper (fig. 65). In speculating on its appearance if Rodia had conceived it via the drawing-board, we would have to study the effects of graphic vehicles on design. It is this consideration that we turn to next.

Fig. 65: The Watts Towers in Los Angeles. Photo Mike Jenks.

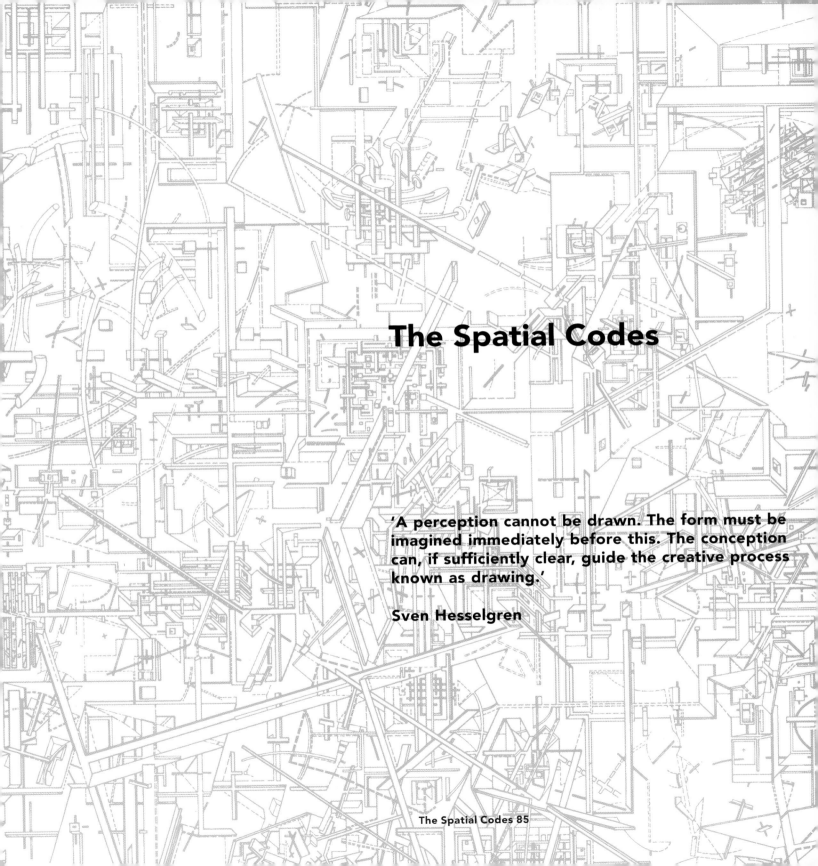

The Spatial Codes

'A perception cannot be drawn. The form must be imagined immediately before this. The conception can, if sufficiently clear, guide the creative process known as drawing.'

Sven Hesselgren

The Spatial Codes

Whenever the environmental designer is confronted by a design problem the initial solving process involves a visualization of potential solutions. The imagination triggers a concept which is imagined ('seen') as a flashing, dimensionless image with the mind's eye - images formed from a creative leap into the proposed environment. These can result from, or be subject to, individual prejudices, intuitions, or a systematic analysis or reduction of criteria. Such a mental picture is akin to a photographic impression - incomplete, in a state of flux and somewhat vague; it originates from many forces at work within the designer's mind including the nature of the immediate problem, personality traits and past experience - many of these latter influences lying beyond any conscious control. These factors continue to have some bearing on decision-making throughout the ensuing and evolving sequence of design.

It might be possible to generate and develop images from concepts in the mind alone. But spatial ideas can become so extensive and complex that they can no longer be contained within the mind and have to be externalized. Representation in some tangible form is necessary so that they can be clarified, assessed and articulated. At this point the idea has to pass through space and (depending on the designer) be translated into two or three dimensions, as a descriptive model which allows the designer to experience the nature of the idea and develop its conception. This perceived experience, newly-represented, of form-space acts as the basis for further development inspiring the creative imagination on to other mental images which are, in turn, realized in representational form for personal or group evaluation. This two-way language of design is a continuous dialogue between concept and mode of expression - alternating until the creative process is exhausted (figs 66 & 67).

Through drawing, the architect has traditionally learned to transfer the shifting images of the mind's eye on to the drawing board.

Fig. 66: Conceptual drawing for the Peckham Library and Media Centre, by Will Alsop.

This kind of visualization technique has been commonly accepted as an invaluable design tool and considered as having little effect on the final appearance of architectural form. For example, in addressing students in the 1930s, Le Corbusier explained that architectural form and space is first a concept of the brain, being conceived with the eyes shut; paper was only a means of transmitting spatial ideas back to the designer and others.

Conceptual Diagrams

The moment an idea is transferred from a designer's mind to an external form is a critical point in the life of any architectural design concept. In order to give birth to the idea the designer must adopt some form of abstraction which represents or reflects the pictures in the mind. The process of abstraction usually involves a use of embryonic ideograms, descriptive symbols or annotation - images and words which combine to chart the potential relationships between the concept and reality. The diagram appears most useful in these crucial moments for, in functioning as a constructive doodle, it is clearly more concerned with the essence of ideas, than the prediction of appearance.

According to the designer Keith Albarn a diagram is evidence of an idea being structured - it is not the idea but a model of it, intended to define its characteristic features. He writes: 'It is a form of communication which increases the pace of development or allows an idea to function and develop for the thinker while offering the possibility of transfer of an idea or triggering of notions'. He concludes: 'through appropriate structuring, it (the diagram) may generate different notions or states of mind in the viewer.' However, these different 'notions or states of mind' are susceptible to three factors which are also rooted in the designer's mind - first, familiarity with the mode of expression, then the amount of information that it supplies and, embracing all, the previous experience of three-dimensional space.

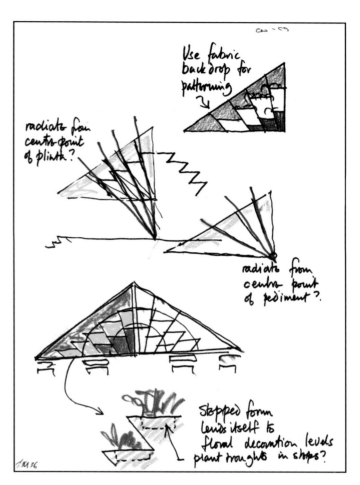

Fig. 67: Conceptual sketches for the entrance to Clifton Nurseries, Covent Garden, by Terry Farrell

In order to develop an effective design model and facilitate the evolution of forms in response to this model, a variety of diagrams - each with their own potential and conceptual set of rules which aid decision-making - may be employed:

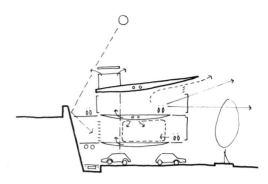

Schematic or Synthetic Diagrams are simplified drawings of a concept which stress the relationships and orientation of its physical components. They help the designer to articulate physical forms in response to specific forces such as air and sun movements and views, etc. These types of diagram are usually composed by annotating a schematic drawing with graphic symbols which represent the idea underlying the form. Orthographic or axonometric drawings are frequently employed in this capacity to portray the concrete image, which is then subject to an overlay of the abstract idea (fig. 68).

Operational Diagrams are examples of another conceptual model which aid the designer in visualizing changes in time. They begin to explain the mechanics of a concept, how its elements are manipulated and transformed, and include 'exploded' and 'x-ray' drawings and thumbnail axonometrics and perspectives (fig. 69).

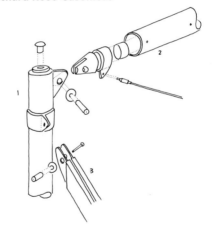

Functional Diagrams identify the proximity and relative size of zones of activity. They are usually called 'bubble diagrams' and represent the plan in embryo for, as they evolve, the bubbles can metamorphose into definite shapes. These are then dimensioned and given openings - the resultant plan then being vertically extruded and given a lid before being re-examined in other graphic modes. This process is a kind of design sequence in miniature - a route in which the archetypal doodle plays a major role (fig. 70).

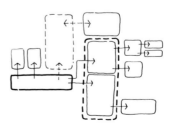

Flow Diagrams are, like their 'operational' counterparts, four-dimensional in that they can identify changes over time. They are often used to study direction, intensity, conflicts, problems and possibilities that arise when movement is considered between one point and another, for example pedestrian movement, transport, information, air and water currents. These diagrams can be used in the abstract or superimposed over other drawings when relating information (fig. 71).

Analytical Diagrams are useful in visually identifying and relating design constraints which have an influence on an evolving conception. Their salient function lies in the investigation of the nature of existing conditions, such as the proposed site for a building, and the evaluation of a completed design in comparison with its original intentions (fig. 72).

Such diagrams tend to initiate a design process which many architects describe as a 'journey'. For some, the diagram points the way into previously unexplored territory, an enterprise accompanied by the thrill of the unknown. Others employ diagrams to chart a route toward a vague conception of the outcome already envisioned in the mind's eye. However, en route, they all encounter quite different types of apprehension, with interludes of reflection and criticism separating periods of rapid and intense activity in which new questions and new ideas are thrown up. As the initial scribbles on paper prepare the way for the further development of ideas - involving the introduction of the cross-section and the elevation as a check on the diagrammatic stage - the next drawing stage sets out concepts more formally. During this stage in the 'journey' drawings can be overlaid and mixed together, the type of drawing being selected to correlate with the problems encountered. Different frames of mind can also involve different drawing mediums for producing and representing ideas. But, as Bryan Lawson points out in his book, *Design in Mind*, there is also the ever-present danger of designers becoming seduced by their own drawings, that is, designing the drawing rather than the building.

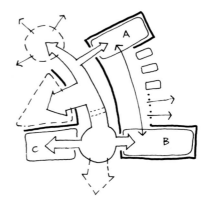

Figs 71 & 72: Examples of flow diagrams (above) and an analytical diagram (below). Courtesy Richard Rose-Casemore

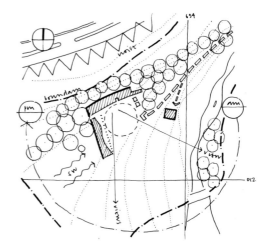

Concepts as orthographics

Being conceptual abstractions, the plan, section and elevation reflect a series of vantage points from which the mind's eye can scrutinize the relationships between the solid and void of an idea. Both the plan and the section function as scaled incisions: the former being made in a horizontal plane and visualized directly from above, the latter made in the vertical plane and 'seen' in parallel with the ground plane. The elevation visualizes external appearance produced on the vertical plane by the projection of parallel sight lines.

The resulting set of orthographic drawings represent the convention of orthographic projection. It is immediately evident that these spatial codes can only convey physical dimensions because they disregard any dynamic relationship in terms of distance from the object, movement around it and our viewing inclination. Within the traditional mode these drawings are, more often than not, drafted in monochrome and in line and retain a diagrammatic quality throughout. Quite apart from the obvious absence of such primary cues as binocular vision and movement parallax, many secondary cues are also missing, for example, apparent size given by light and shadow or the inclusion of background information. Similarly, tonal shading would give a linear perspective. Visual characteristics such as surface quality, texture or colour are not accounted for, but many architects will render such drawings to intensify their images (figs 73 & 74).

John McKean has described the use of the plan and the section as a 'conventionalized system for describing relationships, for showing how the instrument of architecture will be: how it will allow or forbid, encourage or inhibit behaviours'. He concludes: 'it (orthography) is no more to do with the visual than are equations or a published novel (blind mathematicians, novelists or space planners experience similar problems).'

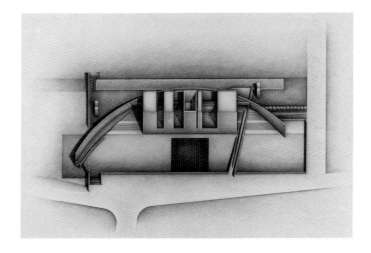

Figs 73 & 74: Two rendered plans for Takamatsu's Shoji Ueda Museum of Photography, which comprises four small blocks linked by a curved exterior concrete wall that echoes the nearby Mount Daisen.

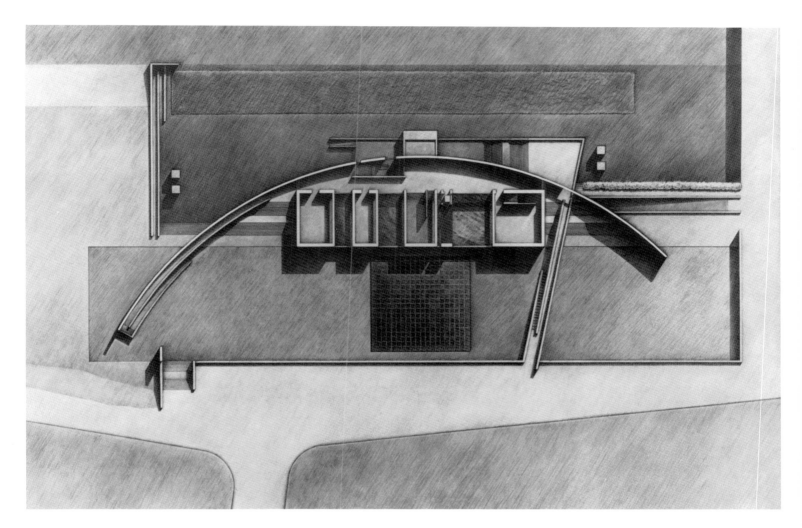

As early as 1957 Bruno Zevi argued that architectural space is not
adequately represented by designers, and that this was due to
the fact that, compared with technological advances in sound
and image reproduction, the graphic language of architecture is
isolated and archaic. Although the plan is still the sole means at
our disposal for evaluating the architectural organism as a whole,
he defines it as an abstraction entirely removed from any real experience; he blames Le Corbusier who, in promoting the plan as
the design generator, encouraged its mystique and endorsed its
primacy in design.

Zevi proposes that its traditional rendition could be improved
and, as black more readily attracts the eye than white, that a

Fig. 75: Detail of a
painting by Will Alsop.
Photo Roderick Coyne

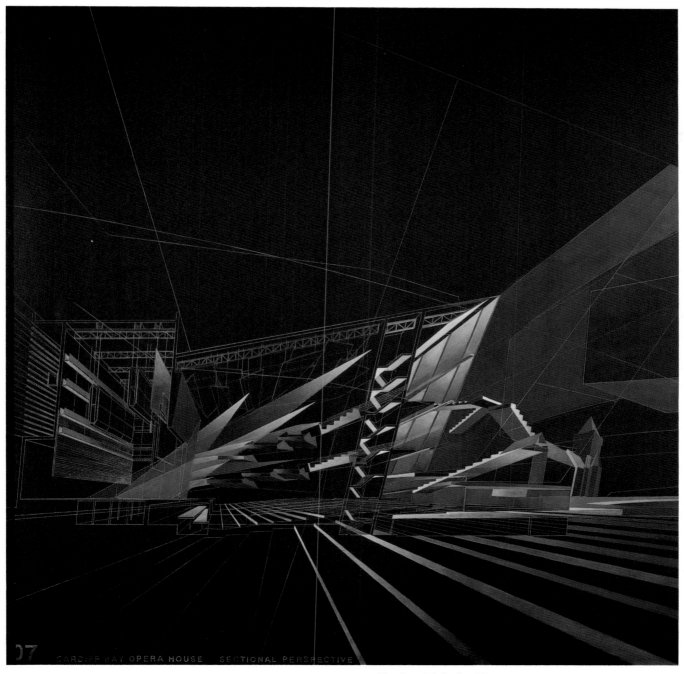

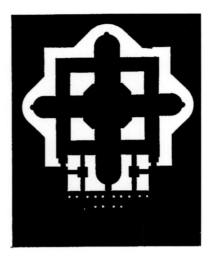

graphic negative of the common black-on-white plan drawing
makes the first step toward a more spatially meaningful representation. In so doing, we move away from the plan as an isolated
container of interior space because, in order to complete the
negative figure, we are now committed to defining it as a conceptual articulation of both interior and surrounding exterior
space. This form of representation, he suggests, responds to the
simultaneity of its original conception, that is portraying 'inside'
and 'outside' not as separate, disconnected entities, but as a coherent and interdependent space emanating from a singular
inspiration (figs 77 & 78).

Zevi then moves to graphic articulation of the space within the
building design. This involves a totemic graphic structuring of the
hierarchy of space which formally accounts for the nature of its
changing dynamic in the vertical plane. Although these spatial interpretations are incomplete in themselves, Zevi concludes that
they move us closer to the heart of the problem of space and its
planimetric representation (fig. 79). Furthermore, although we
may never succeed in discovering a method of fully depicting a
conception of space in plan, the investigation of the problem of
its rendition is broadened along these lines.

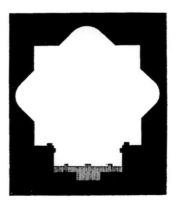

Fig. 79: The plan as a projection of the fundamental structure and as a spatial interpretation. (Plans based on Michelangelo's design for St Peters.)

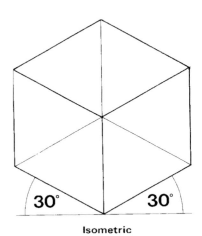

Isometric

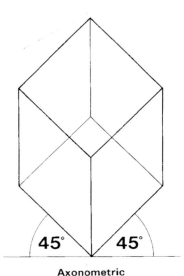

Axonometric

Fig. 80: Schematic views of isometric and axonometric projections.

Axonometric Projection

Axonometric and isometric projections are drawings from which the third dimension is inferred - the physical dimensions of length, breadth and height are recorded within one projection. In axonometric drawings the effect of depth is obtained by adding the third dimension - usually to a plan. The plan is set at an angle of 45 degrees to the horizontal and heights extruded vertically. In isometric drawings the plan is drawn with its axes at 30 degrees from the horizontal, so that linear measurements are the same but angles are distorted. Heights are extruded vertically as in axonometrics (fig. 80). This ability to convey simultaneously an illusion of three dimensions enables spaces to be organized in volumetrics rather than by area. But isometrics and axonometrics should not be considered as analogous to visual perception (see page 100). Isometric viewpoints are monocular, static and fixed. Again, aerial perspective may be represented but linear perspective is ignored - the form-space retaining its size without any concession to foreshortening (although this could be seen as some compensation for constancy scaling). In linear form, these projections appear devoid of all cues to depth apart from that of overlap but they compel powerful sensations of space. However, this compulsion is in our mind's eye and results from its conditioning to the parallelogram or rhombus as a rectangular plane

Fig. 81: Computer generated image for Will Alsop's Institute of Contemporary Arts project in London. Courtesy Steve Bedford, Virtual Artworks.

seen as occupying space - for even when all depth cues are absent, the parallelogram continues to retain the illusion of its spatial meaning.

Because of their inherent abstraction, axonometric and isometric projections are exclusively employed as containers for ideas. If used for transferring objective information - especially curved or spherical figurations - the distortion encountered in drawing such three-dimensional forms within the rigidity of this projection proves extremely difficult (fig. 82). Therefore, as a developing concept is less resistant to its configuration, we can begin to understand that such a rectilinear overlay on a complex and curvilinear concept could straitjacket any nonconformist idea in embryo. Indeed, when later removing the box construction lines (thus removing the parallelograms) the designer risks divesting the projection of its spatial meaning and increasing the distortion.

A set of orthographic drawings evidence the climax of the conceptual journey and equate to the level of information we can expect in a design process (see page 101). In order to re-experience a concept presented in orthographics we have to translate the drawings by mentally co-ordinating the plan with the section and elevations, the isometric or axonometric providing a single, distorted glimpse of its third dimension.

This mental co-ordination of single view drawings can induce a fragmented approach to spatial organization. For example, it can lead to separate level design in planning space; an attitude in which a concept is considered as a number of layers - a stack of sandwiches - each conceived independently, with the elevations functioning as wrapping-paper to bind them together, so that elevations are seen as individual planes, unrelated to other surfaces and disconnected from interior space. But, as we have already hinted, our built environment is most at risk from a further side-effect, that of squareness, an effect that relates to our apparent

Fig. 82: A design concept for a circular stage by Laszlo Moholy-Nagy encased within an isometric container. Courtesy Bauhausarchiv.

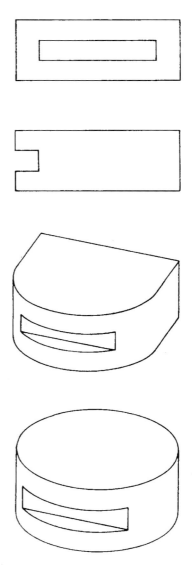

inability to visualize forms which exist beyond the influence of the right-angle. This was demonstrated by Victor Papanek who, in his book *Design for the Real World*, described an experiment in which students were asked to interpret the information provided by a front and side elevation (fig. 83). Due to its ambiguity two solutions are possible and Papanek found that more architects and draftsmen failed to arrive at the more 'elegant' solution (the lower version) than those uninitiated into orthographics. Because of the lack of depth cues in the elevations, the designer/ subjects had assumed that they described a squareness or rectangularity - being unable to visualize alternative forms.

The elevations used in Papanek's test belong to the ambiguous language of spatial codes - a language which makes it difficult for its user to conceive of space other than that complementary to its descriptive powers. At its worst, the Modern Movement's infatuation with a simplistic philosophy has often resulted in monotonous solutions, but orthographic projection may be as much to blame. At best, we can find examples of its effect in the work of more creative designers. For example Walter Gropius, in designing the interior of the Director's office in the Weimar Bauhaus, expressed a design philosophy which appears inextricably linked into the mechanics of an isometric. The horizontal planes in Frank Lloyd Wright's designs seem to derive their pleasure from elevation drawing, and the sawn-off appearance of several of Paul Rudolph's earlier buildings betray an enjoyment of exposing their inner cells in the manner of the cross-section (fig. 86). According to Charles Jencks, 'Stirling's work is rooted in his techniques of drafting: the method leads to the form'. The late James Stirling's love of minimal, deadpan axonometrics speaks for itself - the edges of his buildings closely following the angles and axes of their initial representations (fig. 87). However, the potential of any three-dimensional idea in flux requires a more dynamic articulation than the single, static view used by many designers.

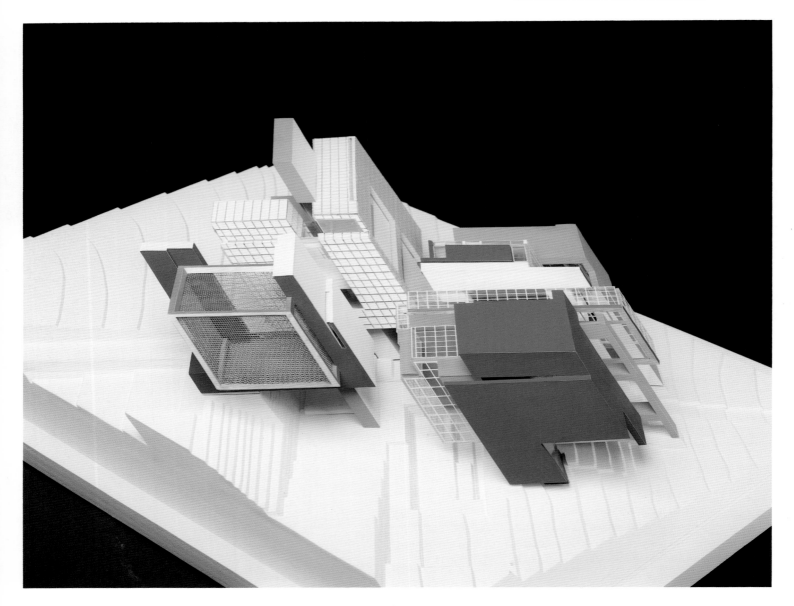

Fig. 84: This model for Peter Eisenmann's House X projects an axonometric drawing into three dimensions to make tangible its inherent distortion. Photo Dick Frank Studio.

Fig. 85: Conventional orthographic display of a design for a control tower, comprising plan, section and elevation by the unconventional Philippe Starck

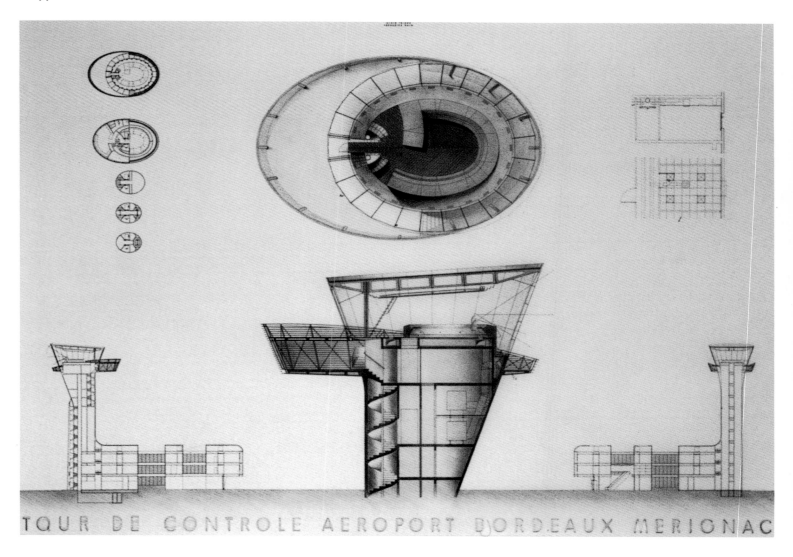

TOUR DE CONTROLE AEROPORT BORDEAUX MERIGNAC

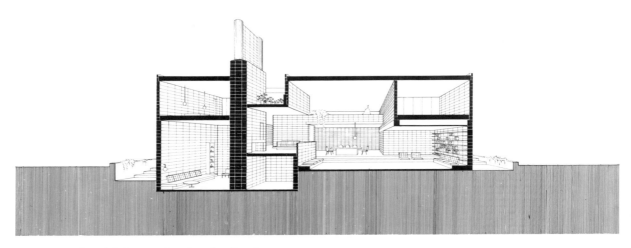

Fig. 86: Paul Rudolph's section drawing for the
Milam residence (above).

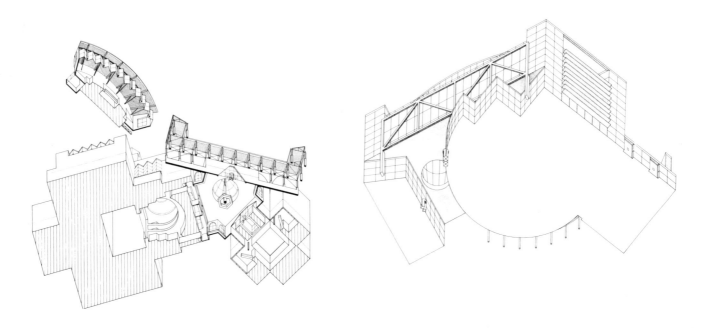

Fig. 87: Two drawings by James Stirling
showing his use of up-view axonometric
projection.

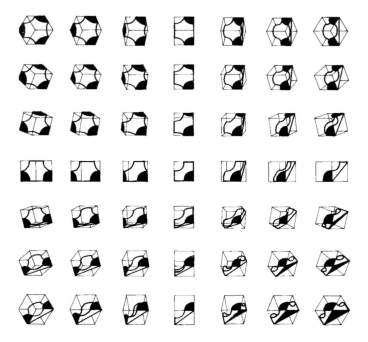

Dynamic Graphics: Concepts in Motion

If we want to appreciate a concept fully we need to experience it from all sides and at all angles, turning the object in our mind before its transfer to and articulation in graphics. For the purpose of an animated perception, varieties of isometrics and, indeed, perspectives are employed - their frames of reference or vanishing points being mobilized through sequential drawings which assess the implications of an idea in the round.

For instance, in a documentary on his life and work, the sculptor, Henry Moore acknowledged the range of drawings required to account adequately for more intricate forms. He described his need to create for a single sculpture up to 40, 50, or even hundreds of drawings to convey its complexity. He was, for example, motivated by the interplay of space and form generated by an elephant's skull. The designer, Keith Albarn has also suggested the importance of investigating ideas more fully and in a range of sizes, and devised a basic design teaching method for the all-round analysis of a cuboid concept. He describes a backing-sheet containing different orthographic views of a cube shape: at the top-left a square (the one face elevation), at top-right and bottom-left a rectangle divided by a line (two double-face elevations), and at bottom right a hexagon with three divisions (isometric view). Design ideas can be worked on an overlay sheet and related to the four views. He suggests that this simple, four-stage 'turning' process of architectural ideas is a two-dimensional representation of a three-dimensional representation of a four-dimensional reality (figs 88 & 89).

Historical attempts at recording movement on the two-dimensional plane include the multi-legged, running bison of prehistoric cave painting; the 'echo' lines of animated objects in strip cartoons, and the nude, in the time-exposure of Marcel Duchamp's perception, descending a painted staircase. Central to this development in modern art was the Cubist style, acclaimed as a new

Figs 88 & 89: A sculpture student's design concept tested 'four-dimensionally' in a range of isometric views (above) and Dutch group notnot's similar system derived from a computer model.

vision that redefined perceptual form in painting and created a new language of liberated expression that could make a composite image of a total experience. In its Analytical phase, the appearance of an object in actual space was directly transposed piece by piece into pictorial space. However, once Cubism became disassociated with its strictly representational purpose, it began to flounder. As the movement reached its Synthetic phase, its attention was diverted towards a subjective identity and, despite the efforts of Picasso, its later content seems naive and unconvincing when compared with contemporary developments in the theatre, film and, especially, in computer technology.

Ideas in Perspective

There are many books which deal with perspective. The majority describe its underlying principles through a presentation of its linear projections. The convention of perspective projection is based upon the way in which the human eye perceives parallel lines as converging with distance. This representation of linear perspective, as a constant relationship between apparent size and distance, is normally constructed showing horizontal lines subject to convergence while vertical lines remain constant. Perspectives are generally associated with visual experience as opposed to the physical organization of designed space. Although lacking primary cues to depth, they can lend themselves to more pictorial illustration (shading, texture, colour) and utilization of the secondary cues more than other drawings (fig. 90). However, when compared with visual perception, perspectives do not accommodate for constancy scaling for - like a photograph - they only represent the retinal image on the eye and not the brain's compensatory modification for distance. Thus restricted to a single, static view, perspective is strictly valid for a one-eyed perception - fixed by its monocular co-ordinates.

A perspective drawing provides a small conical or pyramidal view within our hemisphere of vision although the size of a drawing

Fig. 90: Perspective drawing by Wells Coates of his Isokon Flats in London showing his use of textural shading to intensify the depth illusion.

and the assumed proximity of an observer can both affect the degree of simulation. When using them in sketch form, design ideas can be influenced by a need to compose pleasing images on paper - thus contorting a concept and misleading the designer. This graphic form of misrepresentation includes the infamous artist's impression which can convey a dreamworld distortion to both the unwitting designer and an innocent public. Graphic seduction extends far beyond the colourful impressions of the holiday hotels (even if unbuilt or incomplete) of the glossy travel brochure, and the contrived perspectives of desirable property column dwellings - it can exist on the architect's drawing-board where the author is the one deceived.

Accurate perspectives are often easier to construct from viewpoints whence, in reality, the space would never be viewed. This is particularly true of interiors where the vantage points are either located outside the space with one wall removed or, if inside, with the observer impossibly built into the wall. So there is an evident danger of the designer being encouraged, not only to visualize spaces from exterior points, but also fashion ideas from unlikely stances (fig. 91). And, as the laws of convergence in linear perspective are commonly applied to only horizontal lines, the designer may disregard vertical convergence - three point

Fig. 91: This perspective drawing by Coy Howard and Sherwood Roper has one wall cut away in order to gain visual access to the interior.

perspectives rarely being employed. Parallel verticals appear as correct in perspectives of low buildings but when applied to tall buildings they appear rather strange. In consequence, it might be argued, architects adept at stylized perspectives which ignore vertical convergence have a predilection for a squat horizontal architecture.

Apart from the use of perspective drawings in communicating re-solved design ideas, possibly their greatest asset is their speed and ease of production in sketch form at conceptual stages. They are often of use to the designer who needs rapid visual feedback. The need to develop a personal approach in their use, therefore, is important because many such drawings fail to show more than the skeletal starkness of technical drawing. However, as with all graphics, their powers of spatial communication, at whatever stage of use, are positively linked to their translation capacity - both of the mind's eye of their creator and that of any subse-quent beholder!

In comparing the communication prowess of perspective draw-ings and models, an experiment at the School of Architecture, Oxford Brookes University produced some interesting results. Groups of student subjects were first set the task of translating (without representational aids) ten verbally instructed stages in the dissection of a cube. Each stage described an increasingly more complex cut, necessitating the mental retention and contin-ued turning of the impression in the mind's eye. At the stage when unaided visualization broke down the subjects were handed a block of Plasticine and a knife. A second test examined the comparative strike-rate of success as between unaided, graphic and model sequences.

The findings demonstrated that both graphical and physical models had outstripped the progress of unaided visualization. However, in all cases, use of a three-dimensional model enabled subjects to complete the entire sequence quickly and correctly. Consequently, it can be speculated that, if graphic techniques are the sole method employed in design, alternative solutions which might exist beyond their capacity could remain hidden or even ignored. This supposition is reinforced by the documented observations of many design tutors who find that their students tend to be more spontaneously diverse in their ideas and accelerated in their development when working in three dimensions.

Graphic modes of spatial representation can break down when faced with complex forms - there is a redundancy point at which creative designers turn to other media. For example, Louis Kahn, himself an influential draftsman, realized the limitations of perspective views whilst attempting to describe a complicated structure of tetrahedrons and turned, instead, to the medium of models. The use of physical models as a design tool is central to the work of a majority of leading architects; among the more well known being the huge corrugated cardboard block models which appear in the wake of Frank O. Gehry's innovative formal investigations. In discussing the way in which architects tend to solve problems partly as a consequence of the way that they look at their designs, Ian Ritchie rejects the idea of making decisions based solely on drawings. For him the traditional drawing and the physical model are complementary; the model, although not allowing visual access at human scale, providing an overview seen from many directions that a drawing cannot.

Concepts as Scale Models

Depending upon their stage of use and application within a design process, architectural models fall into various types. For instance, the conceptual model is a three-dimensional diagram fabricated when an idea is still fragile. In its basic form, it can be seen in operation at the dining-table when, in earnest conversation, people spontaneously use condiments and cutlery to illustrate a topographical point under discussion. Similarly, in design, physical diagrams are usually constructed quickly with junk or mixed-media to symbolize the components and relationships of an idea. On the other hand, block models carve the external mass of an idea and can include a study of its implications in relation both to the site-space and to that of surrounding mass. By contrast, skeletal models examine functional determinants in isolation from surrounding features. They can act as three-dimensional bubble diagrams in studying activity zones; or physical working drawings in studying structure, assembly, or service systems. The space model articulates the interaction of plane and surface in both interior and exterior, individual or sequential space. More sophisticated versions are employed in simulating natural or artificial lighting conditions. Presentation models represent the total composition of an architectural solution and communicate its finality to others. They take the form of miniature prefigurements of an architecture represented in detail and as a complete entity (figs 92 & 93; see also pp.116-117). Being primarily built for promotion rather than decision-making they are less flexible than the rest and are usually intended to convey qualities of external form and its relationships. More complicated knockdown versions can also be presented so that a closer examination of their internal workings can be achieved.

By working directly in space, albeit at small scale, concepts are formed and reshaped as a result of their exploration in three dimensions; a process in which options remain open in design routes - options which might not appear available to the designer trapped within the confines of paper. However, one significant drawback of scale models is their rich displays of spatial intricacy which can sidetrack the designer into a fascination with 'miniaturism' - an attitude associated with the discrepancy between human and model scales. This effect puts the designer outside the concept by interposing a distance known as the 'Gulliver Gap'.

Figs 92 & 93: Two models by Craig Downie of Studio Downie showing the development of design ideas from a preliminary concept model to a final presentation model.

Artists are fully aware of the fact that the significance of an idea in cartoon or maquette form may be lost or reduced when enlarged to full-size; as the scale of a painting, sculpture, and a building is increased, so the amount of information within the field of vision reduces proportionally - often relegating a seemingly exciting idea to the mundane. As a means of surmounting the scale barrier some architects use a modelscope which transports the mind's eye directly into the model space. Modelscopes are miniature periscopes which, when inserted into models, provide selective and realistic images. Movement through model-space can also be simulated by the simple operation of panning and tracking. These views can be photographed by attaching a camera but the resulting circular photographs tend to be rather poor quality with distortion occurring around the edge (fig. 94).

Model-Video Simulation

In the light of the statement by the psychologist, J.J. Gibson, that a motion picture is 'much richer in information than a still picture', the idea of attaching a video camera to a model periscope as a means of transporting the eye on an animated exploration of the spaces inside and outside scale models provides architects with one means of being able to 'walk around the drawing-board'.

Although the eye is often compared with a camera lens there is an enormous difference between the two. For instance, our eyes are capable of perceiving movement in terms of clearly defined images without the aid of a shutter. The research of Gunnar Johansson of the University of Uppsala, Sweden, concentrated on this remarkable optical operation in which the eye effortlessly decodes the blur of light streaks entering the retina into a structured perception of space and form. He believes that from an evolutionary standpoint this ability was a necessary part of our biological survival kit for, even in many lower animals, a similar dependence on changes in visual stimulus can be demonstrated.

Fig. 94: View through a modelscope, showing the edge distortion problem.

He cites as evidence experiments in which an image that is mechanically held motionless on the retina seems to fade and disappear. Conversely, our ability to determine visually the precise spatial position of fast moving objects testifies to the fact that the eye is primarily an instrument for analysing changes in light flux over time rather than an instrument for recording static images. Although visual information interacts with signals from other sense organs, other experiments have shown that the visual perception of motion is able to override conflicting spatial information from other channels.

Bridging the Gulliver Gap

It was J.M. Anderson and H.E. Odling who, in conjunction with the University of Glasgow television service in the early 1970s, did much pioneer work in developing this approach to design. Their research was based on the basic limitations of the commercial modelscope which, when used by the naked eye to view models, cannot isolate and focus upon particular aspects of a design and induces the Gulliver Gap - a term originally coined by Anderson. It refers to the 'toytown' syndrome - the awareness of our own physical size in relation to that of a scale model, experienced even when peering down the thin tube of a periscope. The need to both eradicate this unhappy intrusion in design and develop a method of exploring models so that their fuller implications might be made more realistic and accessible to others led to some exciting research.

After linking a camera and a modelscope, mounted together on an overhead movable gantry, a series of tests were conducted to determine the integrity of the televised image in conveying a sense of space. In order to check responses, different groups of subject/observers were asked to estimate a series of dimensions such as heights, widths and depths from a televised image of a real room, and a televised image of a scale model of the same room. It was significant that the subjects generally displayed a high rate of success in determining spatial dimensions particularly from televised pictures of model spaces and, more particularly, that those who had no knowledge of the real space (Mackintosh's Board Room at the Glasgow School of Art) or of the nature of the experiment universally accepted the model simulation as a real space (fig. 95)! In this way, Anderson and Odling demonstrated that it was possible to show observers a convincing and dynamic picture of an architectural space before construction, thus bridging the Gulliver Gap.

Although the television screen is a universally acceptable viewing technique with a framework of conventions allowing the isolation, magnification and reduction of images, it cannot replace a visual perception gained by our physical locomotion through actual space. For the perceptual limitations of TV are those of any two-dimensional image which in being flat relies upon the secondary or monocular cues to depth with the addition of real time motion and movement parallax. Also, in a model, the lack of aerial perspective may work against the acceptance of simulation. Furthermore, periscope optics afford only a small field of vision and, in referring to the work of R. Sommer, Anderson points out that much of our experience of architecture is taken from areas beyond our focus of awareness. At any moment, we carry with us a spherical awareness of physical space - half of which is stored as memory in the brain of what exists behind us, while the other half is visible.

In tandem with advances in electronics and fibre-optics, together with research into movement patterns and visual perception which provide yet another laboratory check on our psychology of behaviour in the real world, television and film simulation has refined its visual, tracking and scanning abilities. By the 1980s both private and university-based simulation centres had been established across Europe and America. But, overtaken by a new technology, many of these, such as the Bouwcentrum in Rotterdam,

Fig. 95: The interior of the Board Room at the Glasgow School of Art in a photograph (above) and the onscreen version of the model (below). Courtesy Glasgow School of Art.

have been disbanded. Others have transferred from camera-on-model displays to computer-generated animation, a metamorphosis that takes us back to drawings - but this time those visualized in four dimensions.

Writing in the *Companion to Contemporary Architectural Thought* Cornelius Van de Ven has elegantly described the development of the four-dimensionality of space-time in the artistic hands of the Futurists who, together with Moholy-Nagy and Theo van Doesburg, exercised such a great influence on theoretical thinking. Furthermore, he proposes the general theory that all possible aspects of the representation of space perception can be distilled into the four ways that its illusion can be evoked as defined by El Lissitzky in 1925; namely: '(1) planimetric or two-dimensional space; (2) one-point perspective or three-dimensional space; (3) 'irrational' space-time, or four-dimensional space, and (4) imaginary space as produced by motion pictures'. In conclusion, Van de Ven suggests that: 'our perception of architectural space is, in one way or another, the synthesis of these four phenomena' (fig. 96).

Montage

Van der Ven's reference to El Lissitsky's fourth means of evoking illusions of space, that is, via motion pictures, brings us to a conceptual architectural approach known as 'montage'. Developed in the propaganda photomontages of artists like John Heartfield and George Grosz, in which different photographic stills are collapsed into one to express the unfolding of time, the concept of montage was initially applied to film by the Russian film director Sergei Eisenstein. His cinematic montage was a filmic method of structuring themes and ideas in a juxtaposed and carefully edited sequence of separate pieces or images. He applied it to such films as *Battleship Potemkin*.

Eisenstein explains: 'Montage, in the technical, cinematic meaning of the word, is basic to the cinema; it is deeply grounded in

Fig. 96: Book design by El Lissitzky for Tairoff, *Das Entfesselte Theater***, 1927.**

the conventions of the cinema and in corresponding perceptions of cinema.' Through montage, associations in the viewer are aroused by separate visual elements - montaged pieces - of the analyzed fact. Only in the sum of their experiences do these produce an emotional effect similar to and often stronger than the effect of the fact itself. In his montage of associations an analogous process occurs - in fact, what is juxtaposed is not phenomena but chains of associations connected with the given phenomena which the audience understands in the time sequence.

Eisenstein's process of cutting, editing and piecing together selected fragments of audio-visual material not only anticipated a twentieth century sensibility epitomized in the modern and multi-faceted imagery of a modern television ad or pop video, it introduced a means of communication in real time that comes close to the manner in which we perceive spatial events.

Furthermore, Eisenstein likened his cinematic montage technique to a perambulatory architectural experience; he found a subconscious use of sequential montage in the design of historic buildings such as medieval cathedrals and Renaissance and Baroque churches. However, he was particularly fascinated by August Choisy's account of walking about the Acropolis in Athens (fig. 97). Eisenstein wrote of this: 'It is hard to imagine a montage sequence for an architectural ensemble more subtly composed, shot by shot, than the one which our legs create walking among the buildings.'

Faint echoes of this perceptual architectural perambulation can be detected in the up-view axonometric drawings of the late James Stirling (see page 102). Also influenced by Choisy, these allowed his mind's eye to penetrate the complex sequencing of his unfolding volumes and spaces. Stronger echoes are found in the drawings and models of Richard Meier whose museum designs embody a montage of gradually disclosed transparency.

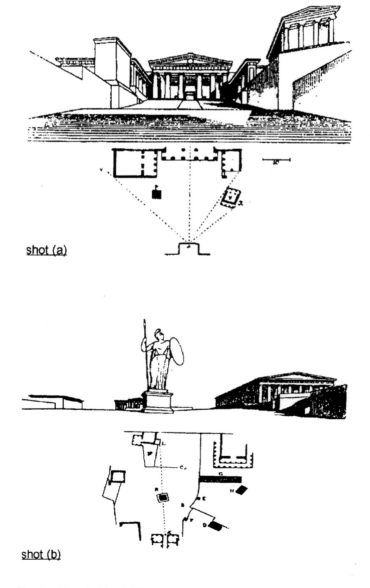

shot (a)

shot (b)

Movement through his museums set in motion the overlapping transparency of objects and parts of the building, while the overlapping of primary geometrical forms rotate and displace to create spatial diversity and complexity at every step. Both Stirling's and Meier's montage approach finds roots in what Le Corbusier described as the 'promenade architecturale', that is, architectural space as perceived by a viewer in motion. In turn, the creation and understanding of three-dimensional space through the viewers ability to montage sequentially multiple visual events transposes a Cubist deconstruction into the real time of architectural experience. Moreover, it represents an almost cinematic design approach.

A more direct link between architectural design and film-making is found in the practice of Rem Koolhaas. He sees his role as architect as being more like a scriptwriter or film director who conceives architectural episodes and episodic sequences which, being suspenseful over time, build up to a climax of spatial experience. Steeped in a design philosophy which celebrates a 'culture of congestion' involving overlapping meanings and alternative realities, he describes the process of making architecture as one very similar to that of making movies. Indeed, derived from distinctive generative graphics, his design for the Rotterdam Kunsthal was conceived in serial vision; the route through it being structured like a plot for a movie, that is, with a beginning, a middle and a powerful climax. Movement through this museum is celebrated by bombarding the visitor with a montage of conflicting and quickly changing impressions and, with each turn of the head, surprising encounters. Contrasting functions, the blurring of interior to exterior views, drama in the degrees of transparency and change in level, colour shock tactics plus a deliberate juxtaposition of commonplace and exotic materials to expose their inherent visual and tactile qualities are all combined, 'cut' and 'edited' to heighten sensory awareness and to create the potential for a new architectural expression. Finally it comes as no

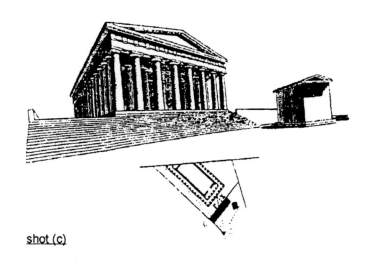

shot (c)

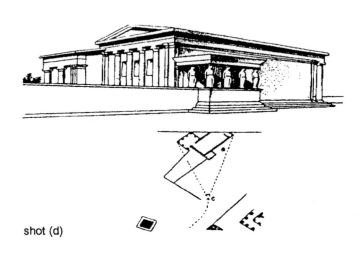

shot (d)

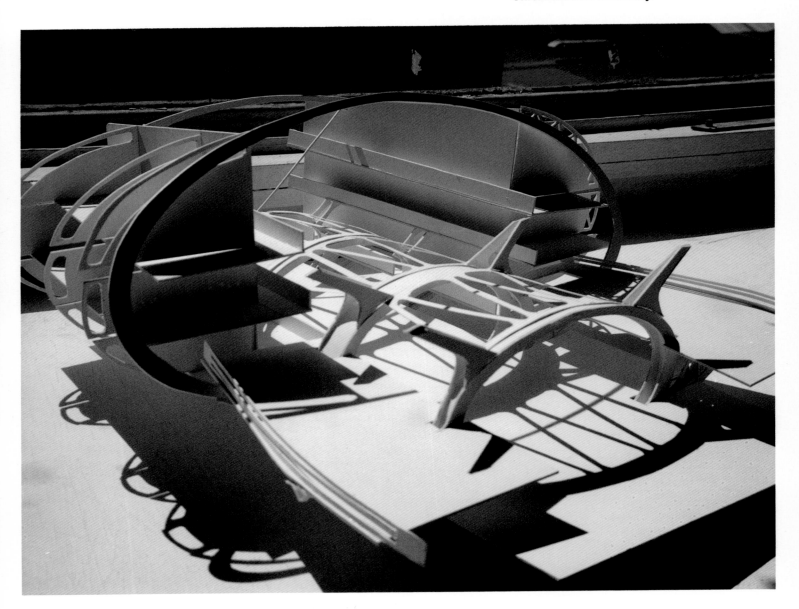

Fig. 99: Presentation model of Will
Alsop's Berlin Embassy project.
Photo Roderick Coyne.

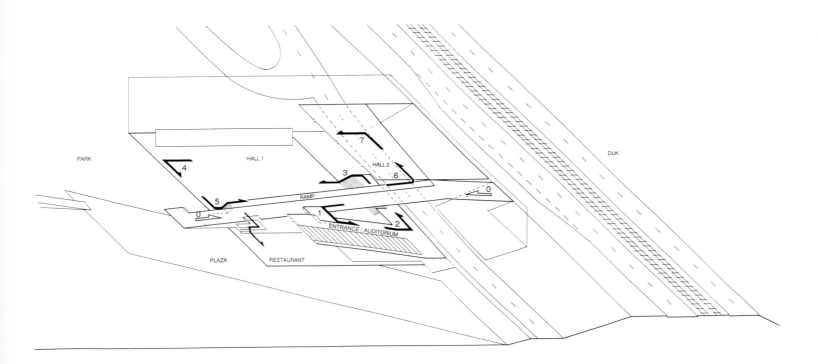

PARK   HALL 1   HALL 2   DIJK

RAMP

ENTRANCE / AUDITORIUM

PLAZA   RESTAURANT

surprise that, before embarking on his architectural career, Koolhaas had, like Eisenstein, studied, directed and acted in films (fig. 100).

As part of his phenomenological design approach - often producing an architecture incorporating non-orthogonal geometries - the projects and buildings of Steven Holl reflect a spatial experience as if in a progression of cinematic stills. He describes our perception of space at any single moment as a simultaneous meshing of three spatial fields: foreground, middle-ground and distant view. Involving form and proportion together with the smaller scale of details and materials and the subjective qualities of surface and light, this composite view forms the basis of a 'complete perception'. He suggests that to design from inception for this concept of time and 'movement space' would be difficult using the traditional plan and section. Furthermore, it would also not be served by the static perspective vanishing point nor the rational space of an axonometric projection. He concludes that 'an infinite number of perspectives projected from an infinite number of viewpoints could be said to make up the spatial field of the phenomena of a work of architecture'. Consequently, our passage through a visualization of architectural space would be

Fig. 100: Rem Koolhaas's design for the lower levels of the Rotterdam Kunsthal shows a circulation pattern based on a filmic serial vision which bombards the visitor with quickly changing impressions.

better considered as a series of cinematic images, i.e., a montage, changing as the head turns. In design terms, this implies a need to create architecture using a series of perspectives - each examining the overlap of different spatial fields. The consideration of form in this manner - from inception to completion - not only gives priority to the bodily experience of the developing space, but it also serves to bind the intention of the architecture with the perception of the perceiver.

Computer Aided Design

Without doubt the representation method which has superseded all previous forms of visualization in the last decade or so is that which involves the computer and its ancillary equipment. Back in the early sixties, the computer found it easier to process information than to present it; the first CAD programmes for architecture involving a slow speed of operation. At that time computers had acquired something of a bad name with architects because few could understand them nor afford them: computers seemed unlikely to be of much use other than as a workhorse for the laborious problems of preparing and checking programmes; also, it was feared that a machine might assume the role of designer or, at least, effect a standardized approach to design. Despite this premature short-sightedness, however, a computer technology harnessed to the architectural design process has developed at a fantastic pace, so much so that not only are many of its latest techniques in search of problems to solve, but it has come to question the very nature of our perception.

Wireframe drawing is where CAD began; creating fine line structures in flickering green on black screens. It remains the underlying function of most CAD programmes which offer the option of assembling an initial drawing in two dimensions or in three dimensions. Once the orthographic co-ordinates of a design are fixed in 2D plans, elevations and sections, they can be exported to 3D programmes where, using a carefully planned

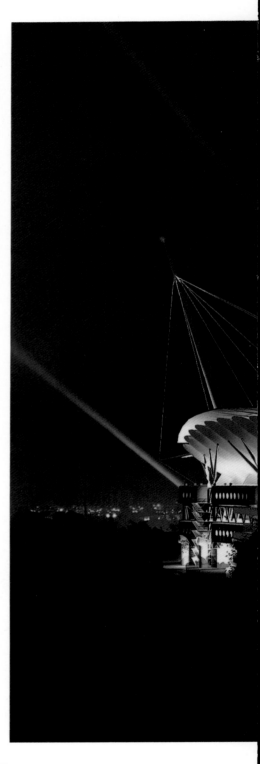

Fig. 101: Computer image
produced by Alan Davidson to
document Richard Rogers' Saitama
Stadium in Japan. This image won
top prize in the 1996 CICA awards.

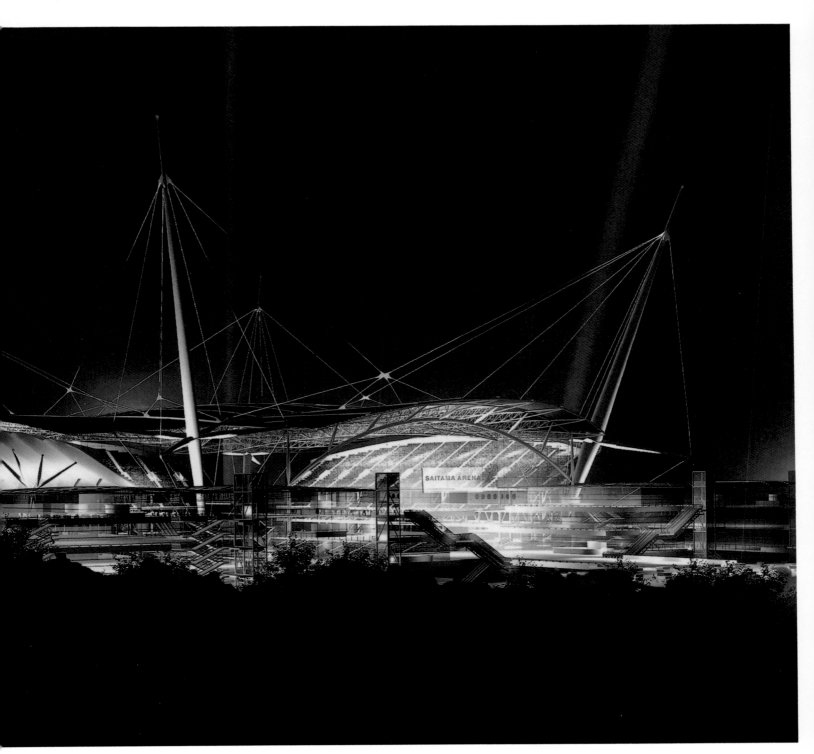

Image text: SAITAMA ARENA

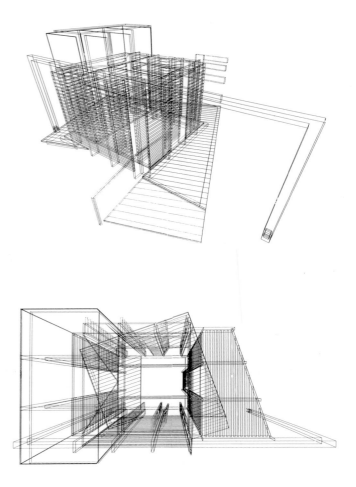

layering system, the machine plots the relevant position of end points for their integration into a virtual three dimensional space (fig. 102). The resultant white or multicoloured wireframe perspective provides a valuable first glimpse of a skeletal structure defined in abstract form. Often used as a check on initial ideas previously sketched on the drawing-board, many students and practitioners will have the machine assemble them with the hidden line routines omitted so that all the underlying levels of information are simultaneously in view; the resultant image providing a stance which many designers find to be the ideal interface between the physical aspects of a design and the abstract ideas that underpin it. In addition to this ability to examine a project using a see-through, x-ray vlsion, there is the attendant ability to command a myriad of possible and, indeed, impossible vantage points from which to generate the views. This provision allows the mind's eye to preview and rehearse the nature of a spatial complex in flux - a perceptual liberation that echoes the montage approach extolled by Koolhaas and Holl. Yet another aspect of this perceptual freedom is the dynamic provided by the three-point perspective view so quickly generated on the screen - a dynamic which has come to supplant the conventional rigidity of those one- and two-point versions laboriously produced on the drawing-board.

When 2D plans and elevations together with the 3D model are exported as files and imported to a second CAD system, such as Modelshop or 3D Studio, wireframes can be rendered and, as the design firms up, have planes and surfaces 'painted' to conceal those parts of the structure not visible from the chosen viewpoints (fig. 103, and see page 120). During this stage - usually later in the design process - the abstraction of the wireframe is fleshed-out with a rendered overlay of spatial elements including colour, shadow effects and surface texture treatments. However, when a rendered CAD sequence becomes animated, the architect becomes 'movie director': lighting becomes orchestrated,

Fig. 102: Two wireframe drawings for Craig Downie's Hat Hill Gallery. Note that the complete frame appears, rather than concealing lines hidden by structures in front.

the architectural 'set' is painted and movement around it is cho-
reographed. The animation sequence can be 'filmed' as a
continuous loop or be open-ended, the final rough cut being
played back at up to twenty-five frames per second. Once filed as
one package, the animation can then be viewed by the architect
and the client. It can be experienced on foot as a walkthrough or
in flight as a flythrough. The result can be experienced in the formal starkness of a block model or in a convincing degree of
resolution which, using today's software such as Graphisoft's
ArchiCAD, Bentley System's Microstation, or AutoCAD Release 5
and 3D Studio Max, which offer 2D and 3D animation in one
package, can produce highly realistic video sequences.

A resolved design can be taken to even greater heights of resolution: photographic source material can be scanned in and, for a
photo-montaged animation, even fully-rendered building proposals
patched into scanned photographs of the site (see page 97). Also,
the incidence of light in a rendered image becomes far more realistic via a technique called 'ray tracing'. Relying upon

**Fig. 103: A rendered design for
building created using AutoCAD 3D
Studio on a wireframe created in
AutoCAD AEC. Courtesy Autodesk.**

Fig. 104: Fully rendered computer image created by Giuliano Zampi for the interior of the Hong Kong Telecom building

sophisticated programming, extensive memory and fast computing times, ray tracing is a process in which all the lines of light visible from the viewer's position are calculated and valued, including light rays passing between objects within a given scene. Even more realistic lighting effects are provided by the radiosity programme, a recent technique which, in creating a virtually realistic pattern of light and shade, highlight and reflection, pushes the illuminated image on the screen to higher and higher levels of realism (figs 105 & 106, and see page 124).

As CAD programmes become increasingly powerful and more complex, and as final-generation systems provide more sophisticated rendering tools, the fact remains that this version of reality is confined to the rectangular glass of the television screen. Despite this drawback, however, the new technologies including television and the computer, have not only brought extraordinary representational prowess to the fingertips of designers, but also shifted dramatically the emphasis from a conventional visualization involving planning and elevating to one in which they can engage with an idea in the round, that is, from within and around the virtual space of its conception. In other words, the architect has shifted from a static design stance to one that is cinematic.

In supplying all the spatial variables intrinsic to moving pictures, the computer-generation of design concepts represents the first step in a new and exciting adventure into visualization. The challenge of recreating a virtual image of a concept in the same virtual space as that occupied by its conceiver now confronts us. To do so, we have to make a creative leap through the television screen and into the world of imagination that lies beyond. Previously the domain of trainee astronauts and video game designers, it is a world that returns us to the full-scale design overtures used by the ancients but this time reconstructed electronically in the space of our minds.

Figs 105 & 106: Two images created by the architect Giuliano Zampi, using Sonata on a Silicon Graphics workstation. These show the high degree of resolution, including diffused lighting effects, achievable with contemporary CAD systems.

Fig. 107: Visualisation of an office
project in Hong Kong created by
Giuliano Zampi.

Full-Size Interaction/Simulation

'All the techniques of representation and all the paths to architecture which do not include direct experience are pedagogically fruitful; but their function is no more than allusive and preparatory to that moment in which we, with everything in us enter and experience the spaces we have been studying. That is the moment of architecture.'

Bruno Zevi

**Figs 108 & 109: Mockups of
rockets and space vehicles at the
NASA Museum at the John F.
Kennedy Space Center, Florida.
Courtesy NASA.**

Full-Size Interaction/Simulation

To be able to take a real-time walk around a full-scale prelude to a building design has been the dream of many architects. In order to accomplish this in the past, several have constructed replicas at a 1:1 scale and this prefabrication of building proposals is still in evidence today. However, a new medium - still in the process of being developed and, indeed, understood - holds implications far beyond the realms of our wildest dreams. Its potential in the design process is one of the most exciting innovations of our time, for the ability to manifest tangibly the fruits of our imagination in three-dimensional space so that we can move around and inside them and share this experience with others is of the greatest interest to the designer.

Concepts to Full-scale

Experimental mock-ups as an evaluative aid to design are usually constructed from materials other than those intended for the ultimate form. For example, Michelangelo prefabricated full-size wooden replicas of parts of buildings such as cornices and had them hoisted into position so that he, and his clients, could assess their suitability before completing construction. Similarly, Sir Christopher Wren had a plaster copy of a piece of sculpture intended for St. Paul's Cathedral positioned on its unfinished edifice in order to examine its visual effect and as a check on its scale prior to the production of further sculpture. In 1972, when Oxford's City Council were considering the re-siting of the Carfax Conduit - a medieval water pump displaced from its original setting in the busy city centre - they had a painted canvas, wood and metal replica made and erected in a newly proposed site (fig. 110). After a period of deliberation, the mock-up was removed. That its new setting would be inappropriate was thus an informed decision.

Canvas and timber was also employed by Mies van der Rohe in the fabrication of a full-sized mock-up of his Kröller House built on its site in the Hague, and Edwin Lutyens prefabricated in wood

Fig. 110: Canvas mock-up of the Carfax Conduit being trialed for its resiting in Oxford's Broad Street. Courtesy Oxford & County Newspapers

his extension to Castle Drogo in Devon, to give his client a preview of its full-scale appearance. In the only remaining
photograph of this extravagant construction - the project was
curtailed in 1930 - the windowed block to the left alone is real, to
the right everything, including the main gateway, has been executed in falsework to study the 'Spartan romantic' qualities of
the castle's hilltop silhouette (fig. 111).

The anticipatory simulation of full-sized architectural space can
take on various forms, being used for different times, for different
purposes and at many stages in the design process. In 1959,
when the Greater London Council were reconsidering a planning
application for the Shell Building, large balloons were floated
above the site-space as a method of identifying the upper limits
of the proposed mass and its effect on the immediate environment. This simple method is commonly employed as an aid in
anticipating the effects of high-rise buildings, for example in the
planning of theme parks in the United States. It is also common
practice for builders to erect a sample panel of brickwork on the
building site for approval by the architect. Similarly, some of the
shell roof units for Jørn Utzon's Sydney Opera House were
mocked-up in wood to full scale but for functional and structural
rather than visual purposes. A common practice in the United
States is the on-site construction of one floor of a skyscraper before building commences, the prototype being utilized for
experiments with lighting, services detailing, colour schemes and
furniture layout (as well as today for marketing multi-occupancy

Figs 112, 113, & 114: Two environments created by Infobyte for ENEL, Italy: two views of the landscape inside Giotto's frescoes (left) and the former basilica of St Peter's in Rome (right).

Full Size Interaction 135

Fig. 115: Mock-up of one level of
Skidmore, Owings and Merrell's
design for the Union Carbide
Building, New York. Courtesy
Skidmore, Owings and Merrill

buildings). As each of the floor spaces of a skyscraper are virtually
identical, this process, economically viable for prestigious buildings, was used in the internal planning of the Seagram Building
and Chase Manhattan Bank and the Union Carbide Building in
New York City (fig. 115).

Mock-ups are also widely used in the development of ships, aero-
planes and spacecraft; the latter process providing a fascinating
junkyard of castoff hardware housed in the NASA museums at
Washington DC and Cape Kennedy, Florida (figs 108 & 109,
pages 130-131). Where mass-production of housing is concerned,
full-size mock-ups of designs for individual units intended for extensive proliferation can enable better public participation in their
creation. One has only to observe the popularity of the site show-
house on real estate developments or the complete houses
erected and then dismantled for Ideal Home exhibitions to realize
their value in communicating with a lay public who find extreme
difficulty in reading architects' drawings.

Depending upon the nature of the mock-up, all visual cues can
be represented in space, obviously providing a high quality of
both visual and tactile information. The mock-up is also capable
of introducing another missing ingredient from architect's drawings - people; the opportunity for the designer to articulate space
against the reactions of intended users. However, the full-size
simulation of architectural space involves large-scale elements
and requires considerable expense, time and space in production. For example, the large workshops once run by Foster
Associates in South London - used to prelude full-scale office interiors and build prototype columns, partitions and suspended
floor systems, etc. - has long been abandoned. Mock-ups are still
used by some architectural practices, such as Nicholas Grimshaw
& Partners, as probes into extremely delicate situations and enlisted extensively by more environmentally sensitive designers
who care deeply about the total implications of their intentions.

Fig. 116: Inside a Boeing flight
simulator

A close relative of this idea is found in existing, highly sophisticated environments resulting from the mating of mock-ups with the computer. In 1970 Ivan Sutherland described his experience with the dynamic computer displays as a 'window on Alice's Wonderland' for, through them, he had 'landed' an aeroplane on the moving deck of a flight carrier and 'flown' in a rocket at nearly the speed of light. In the linking of computer displays to the full-sized mock-up we arrive at a method of simulation used in the training of boat, aeroplane and spacecraft pilots.

Simulators of this kind have become a way of life for a variety of reasons. They offer safety in training, operating flexibility and cost savings that a real-life training programme cannot challenge. One of the obvious attributes of the simulator is its ability to create emergencies that would be hazardous at sea or in the air and fatal in outer space. For example, in flight simulators the weather conditions are controllable so that pilots can be gradually introduced to progressively deteriorating conditions. Modern flight simulators satisfy demands for total realism over the complete flight envelope with a flight deck that exactly replicates the real thing (fig. 116). The faithful mock-up of a flight deck conveys the illusion of immersion in a real world and comprises motion movements, visual flight displays and computer systems. The other human sense fooled by flight simulation is hearing - engine noise and aerodynamic sounds being reproduced over the complete operational and speed range.

The mock-ups of the Lunar Module simulator used by Neil Armstrong and Edwin Aldrin at the Boeing Space Simulation Center in Washington DC to rehearse their descent and landing on the moon's surface used a camera-on-model display system (figs 117 & 118). However, the developmental work of Ivan Sutherland at the University of Utah in 1970 not only resulted in the replacement of camera-on-model displays with computer-generated graphics, but gave birth to a completely new medium.

Fig. 117: Astronauts Neil Armstrong and Edwin Aldrin practising in the lunar module simulator.
Fig. 118 (below) View of the descent stages for the moon landing projected on television monitors within the simulator.

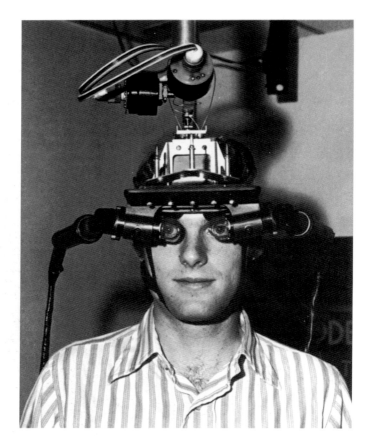

Fig. 119: Pioneer Ivan Sutherland
wearing the prototype helmet

Indeed, his research into flight simulation displays is one of the key antecedents to a completely new and exciting technology which has been compared to Brunelleschi's discovery of perspective and to the invention of television.

Sutherland's dream was to place an observer in the midst of a dynamic computer-generated graphic space and, furthermore, allow the observer to move around and within this real-time perception. His solution was to mount two miniature cathode ray tubes in a headpiece, one positioned in front of each eye (fig. 119). The device was linked to a computer by three aerials which conveyed coordinates locating the position of the wearer's head and direction of view - the display processor instantaneously providing the correct image. Because the stereoscopic apparition remains stationary relative to the observer's movements around the space, the illusion - in this case, a wireframe cube - is present in the room with the viewer. The image appears transparent and presented in glowing green lines - the observer being able to move into appropriate viewing positions in order to examine particular features of the object portrayed. The device, which at the time was in early development stage, would even allow for split-image which, through prisms, permitted the user to view objects overlaid upon the real world.

Although crude and cumbersome, Sutherland's prototype, computer-linked helmet not only gave birth technologically to a new generation of flight simulators, it also heralded a breakthrough in our ability to confront a new version of reality and its representation. Indeed, it had arrived to dissolve the restriction of a Renaissance-imposed picture frame and, as we shall see, enabled us to enter, occupy and explore the world of our imagination.

Virtual Reality: The Second Phase
Beyond the wireframe drawing experienced in real-time through Ivan Sutherland's helmet, and beyond the convincingly rendered CAD walkthrough and flythrough, is the second phase of virtual reality, the stage in which the user and the machine coalesce into a single entity. Around twenty years after Sutherland's pioneer work in Utah a journalist writing for *The Sunday Times* in 1990 described his first excursion into the virtual world: 'All it took was a couple of minutes on an Apple computer, a Lycra glove with sensors to pick up the movements of my hands, a pair of goggles with miniature video screens for lenses, and I flew up a purple chimney'. At the beginning of the 1990s the concept of virtual reality had entered common currency. In the popular media it had been explored, exploited and trivialized in, for example, articles on teledildonics (virtual sex) and in movies such as *Lawnmower Man* and *Johnny Mnemonic*. The new world that had been opened up by the computer and, seemingly, in which anything can happen, is the world of 'cyberspace' (fig. 120).

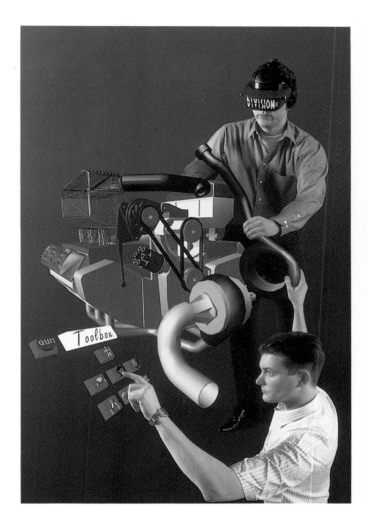

Fig. 120: A visualisation by Division of the potential of contemporary virtual reality

Figs 121 & 122: Two views of projects at Newcastle
Quayside created using Superscape in virtual reality
by Trevor Pemberton and his colleagues at Insite
Environments: Farrell's Ship Inn, below, and a
visitor's centre (facing)

Full Size Interaction 141

The concept of cyberspace was first coined and defined during the 1980s in the novels of William Gibson in which members of a science-fictional, technologically advanced but decaying society plug themselves into global computer networks (fig 123). Quickly adopted in computer jargon, cyberspace describes the conceptual dimension through which electronic information, anything from a phone message to a fax or a photograph to a television signal, is transmitted. In cyberspace data is decomposed or 'liquified' as it is digitally transposed from one medium to another. In this abstract world the building blocks are 'bits' rather than atoms. Using software to order and reorder them, it becomes possible to recreate digitally artificial versions of our physical reality and to construct dreamscapes: imaginary worlds at human scale, or at any desired scale, and with all the traditional notions of reality and conditions of human perception. Moreover, with the aid of the computer, it also becomes possible for us to recreate ourselves and to enter cyberspace and to interact with this digitized environment as freely and directly as we would in the real world.

According to Antonio Caronia, writing in *Ottagono*, the concept of cyberspace has been with us for some time. It simply takes to extreme consequences a process that was already latent in television and computer games where the human imagination becomes suspended between an imaginary, dream-like state and the concrete reality of the everyday experience. It is a convergence where our imagination crashes in upon our physical reality in a most profound way. Thus it is a condition that involves the fragmentation of our body as it trespasses the boundaries of its mental and physical capabilities.

At a basic level, this dissemination of our body or, at least, its organs, has also been touched on by Martin Pawley who describes the way that we use VCRs to watch television without being there, and answering machines to converse with others without lifting the receiver. If television has become an extension of our

Fig. 123: A visualisation still from the film *Johnny Mnemonic*, **screenplay by William Gibson, created using Autodesk's 3D Studio Max.**

eyes, and the telephone an extension of our ears, we can also add the computer as an artificial intelligence existing outside our brain. This 'out-of-body' interface is further extended by 'telepresence', the concept of existing in one place while being in another. Long before the advent of video-conferencing and tele-conferencing we employed robots as virtual body replacements, replicants that, via the computer and using extreme accuracy and precision, repeat our commands and movements while represent-ing us and, in many cases, replacing us in hazardous environments.

However, in the virtual world of cyberspace we take a greater step; we enter a new realm of perception and experience, in which it is possible to cloak ourselves in the simulated body of our choice. Here we can function as ourselves or become superhumans: we can transform into a bird and fly, become an animal or, indeed, an object. Whichever 'body' is selected will simulate our movements or commands to the kinaesthetic princi-ple chosen. There are no limits to this out-of-body experience. Each of these senses can be transposed to another: shapes can become colours, colours tactile sensations, tactile sensations can become sounds, generating a synaesthetic orgy of sensation.

This is a virtual world which, in adapting its initial application in flight simulators, military training and games, is already inhabited by specialist designers such as developmental engineers and re-searchers from several fields including the pharmaceutical and nuclear industries (fig. 124). Using a scale that lies at the opposite ends of a scalar spectrum from that preferred by architects (who traditionally assume Gulliverian proportions in relation to their designs), these designers shrink their virtual selves in order to gain access to the inner space of their prototypes, even down to the molecular level. Once diminished, they make excursions into the virtual space of the three-dimensional working drawings or fully-rendered computer models; they become free to wander, to

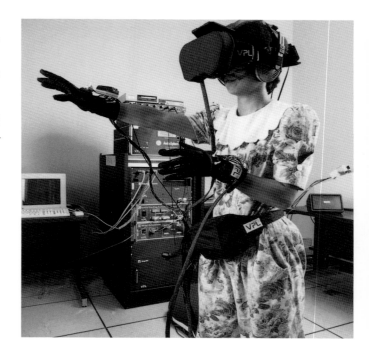

Fig 124: An immersive virtual reality system being tried out at NASA's Johnson Space Center in Houston, Texas. Visual and acoustic information is fed into the headset and phones, while positional information is generated by the datagloves. Courtesy NASA.

Figs 125, 126 & 127: The
Matsushita house project by
Division sought to create a typical
home, in which the placing and role
of electrical and electronic fittings,
and functions such as airflow can be
visually analysed.

check and to fine-tune. Once modified, the designer reverts to normal size, the design updated. The architectural advantages of this technology immediately becomes obvious. For instance, enabling the environmental designer to visualise drawings from the inside, allowing an arena in which to work on a pliable and convincing three-dimensional, real-time model of a concept at full scale, has clear implications for the future of architectural design and its education.

There are two means of access to the world of virtual reality: a non-immersive technology involves pressure-sensitive three-directional mice and stereoscopic screens with special viewing glasses to give a three-dimensional effect, and a fully-immersive technology which, although with us, is still in the stage of developmental flux.

Non-immersive Virtual Reality

A screen-based virtual reality system was enlisted by ENEL (the state-owned Italian Electricity Board) to commemorate their installation of a new lighting system in Giotto's chapel in the Basilica of St. Francis in Assisi. Armed with a special viewing device and a multidirectional mouse, the viewer is able to move about inside an onscreen stereoscopic illusion of the chapel interior, encounter the rich and colourful detail of its architecture and approach and enjoy Giotto's faithfully reproduced frescos which, painted in the fourteenth century, portray scenes from the life of St. Francis of Assisi. But Infobyte, the Italian company commissioned by ENEL to create this virtual image, have incorporated a new and exciting dimension to this 'visit'. Not only can viewers visually explore the subject of each fresco but, by pushing forward on the mouse, they are catapulted into them. What was the two-dimensional picture plane of the fresco becomes a portal through which the 'visitor' is transported to enter the three-dimensional space of Giotto's imagination. What was a planar illusion transforms suddenly into a new version of reality; a habitable world of building, streets and piazzas all reconstructed in Giotto's palette from the visual components seen in the original painting.

In a further project, Infobyte created the interior of the present Papal cathedral of St Peter's in Rome, with its *baldachino* and ceiling frescos. But pass through the end wall, and the visitor stands before Constantine's basilica, which was razed when Bramante's masterpiece was constructed. This work of reconstruction makes a strong case for the value of VR systems not only in imaginative work but also in realising actual, lost buildings (figs 112-114, pages 134/135, and figs 128 & 129).

This newfound ability to make a visual and mental leap into the space of a painting (or the history of a building) and to explore its implied space is the theme of countless short stories. It parallels the creative leap made earlier by the inventors of virtual reality who, in turn, penetrated the looking-glass of a video screen to discover this new world. It is the stuff of fantasy made possible. Indeed, in Salford's new L.S. Lowry Museum, visitors will not only be able to view a collection of his actual paintings but be invited to project their virtual selves through the plane of his canvases and into the three-dimensional naivety of his industrial cityscapes.

Another version of the television screen interface has been developed by the Artificial Life Interactive Video Environment (ALIVE), a collaboration between the Vision & Modelling Group and the Autonomous Agents Group in the Media Lab at the Massachusetts Institute of Technology. Using a magic mirror metaphor, this project takes the form of an enormous screen in which, unencumbered by any ancillary equipment, users confront themselves in a reflected world. There, autonomous elements and animated, programmed characters join the user's own image which, using a video-based tracking system which extrapolates the user's head, hand and body coordinates together with gesture information,

Figs 128 & 129: Two views created by Infobyte, Italy of the cathedral of St Peter's in Rome *(facing)*, **and of the church of St Francis at Assisi** *(above)*.

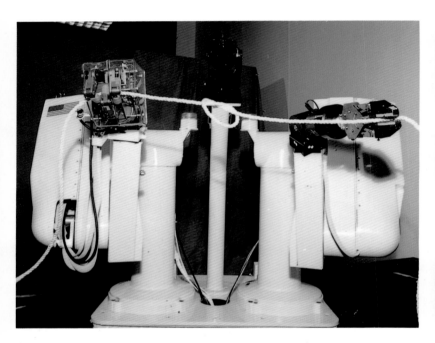
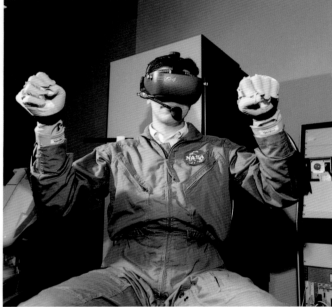

Fig. 130 : The Dart Robotics system
at NASA's Johnson Space Center in
Houston, Texas, uses a virtual
reality system to control a remote
robot. Courtesy NASA.

Fig. 131: Flavia Sparacino's DanceSpace uses a virtual mirror and cameras to create a performance rich in light and colour. Courtesy The ALIVE Group, MIT.

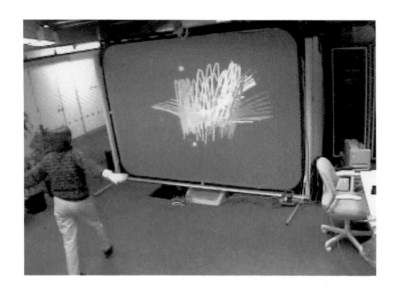

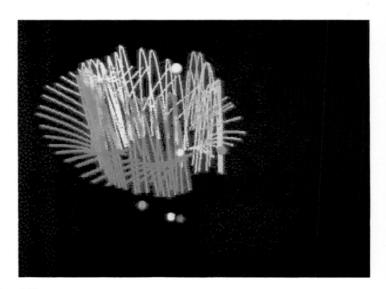

Figs 132 & 133 : Bruce Blomberg's ALIVE system created at the MIT Media Lab uses a set of fixed cameras and a wall-sized screen to create a virtual environment within which he can interact with a virtual, autonomous agent, such as Silas T. Dog, a creature that has learned to react to hand and voice signals.

Fig. 134 (bottom): A further development of the ALIVE environment is to port it into the Doom adventure game: take your virtual dog for a walk in cyberspace! Courtesy Kenneth B. Russell

will respond to the movement and motivation of the user in a believable way (figs 132, 133 & 134).

The convincing excursion into an imaginary, nonexistent or unbuilt architectural event is of tremendous importance to the architect and the artist (fig. 131, page 149). It is further illustrated in the work of William Mitchell and Howard Burns at the Massachusetts Institute of Technology who are establishing a virtual museum of the unbuilt projects of Palladio. A great number of Palladio's designs for villas were never built, and many of those that were have been drastically altered or completely destroyed. Consequently, the museum involves the digital recreation of Palladio's original intentions and will provide any computer on the network with access to three-dimensional models based on schemes published in his *Four Books of Architecture*.

These examples are just a few of the countless project applications which run in tandem with this rapidly advancing technology. Such projects illustrate two important functions of a screen-based virtual reality. First, they function as convincing and engaging presentation devices; second, and more important, they exist as a tool for manifesting and exploring an unbuilt environment.

One project that employs fully both these functions is an ongoing one at Newcastle Quayside where the Tyne and Wear Development Corporation used onscreen virtual reality to design a 25 acre site incorporating offices, retail outlets, leisure facilities, car parking and private housing. Sited on the north bank of the River Tyne close to the Tyne Bridge, the overall masterplan was designed by Terry Farrell & Partners; individual building designs involving other architectural practices such as the Napper Collerton Partnership and Ryder Nicklin. Insite Environments, then called Real Time Design, were enlisted to computer model the site and, as building designs emerged from the masterplan, they become modelled and rendered as separate files and then imported into the main model (figs 121 & 122, pages 140 & 141, and figs 135 & 136).

Being portable, the computer model can be referred to at the monthly monitoring meetings. It is also used in dealings with the local council, community representatives and, of course, for marketing to potential private-sector investors. However, at Newcastle Quayside the ability to visualize a building in advance is a necessary and real part of the creative process of architecture. Individual building designs are examined and studied in the virtual space of their settings and appropriate modifications made. Urban design issues such as massing, circulation, views and disabled access, are also checked according to the findings of walkthroughs and flythroughs.

Figs 135 & 136: Before and after images at Newcastle Quayside, showing how a VR simulation can show in detail the impact of a new building, in this case a pub and restaurant designed by Terry Farrell. Courtesy Insite Environments

Immersive Virtual Reality

Giuliano Zampi and Conway Lloyd Morgan have outlined several distinctions between non-immersive and immersive virtual reality technologies and other active three-dimensional CAD models. By contrast to planned fly and walkthroughs, in true virtual reality the user is autonomous, that is, free from predetermined paths and in complete control of every movement. In non-immersive VR, the user is looking into a screen, whereas the immersive user is actively engaged in the virtual realm. Indeed, the immersive user is part of it, rather than a spectator, even one able to move across and into the screen in all directions. There is a further distinction between the two: the creation of the virtual world requires a powerful computer 'engine' that not only connects the virtual space with the user but is capable of representing to him or her a realistic perspective and polychrome environment which, in real time, responds quickly, accurately and convincingly to every movement made. The quality of this playback relies on programming skill and computer memory, aspects of which are still in the process of development. Immersive VR generally requires more computing power, and so has generally only been available on Unix or Silicon Graphics platforms, while onscreen VR systems can operate on a PC. (This distinction is rapidly eroding at the time of writing, as 16 and 32 MB RAM Pentium PCs become more widely available, and software is being ported from Unix to PC.) Furthermore, immersive users have to carry a set of artificial sensors that replicate a basic array of human perceptions.

In the current state of immersive VR technology the hardware worn is normally a headset and data glove, or three-dimensional mouse. The headset, or Head Mounted Display, familiar in fantasy games, is the main part of this operational system. The headset houses two LCD screens: one for each eye. The addition of earphones to the headset means that the wearer can both participate visually in a three-dimensional and 360-degree experience as well as stereophonically hear virtual sounds. Data gloves embody tactile feedback sensors which, when touching virtual objects or surfaces, transmit equivalent sensations of resistance and plasticity; pointing or clenching the gloved hand conveys commands to the computer so that movement and the manipulation of virtual objects and spaces is possible.

More lightweight displays and tracking systems are now being developed; small goggles and even contact lenses are coming to replace bulky headsets. Full body suits are available, often used by computer animators to record exactly complete body positions. There is also research which aims to perfect voice command recognition and an 'eye-tracking' technology in which playback is projected directly on the retina. In responding to head and eye movements, a newly regenerated perspective stitched together in real time, is received by the eyes thirty times per second. There are also developments, especially in the computer game industry, in which smells and even tastes can be simulated, but this technology is still in its infancy. Using slimmed-down data gloves, the sense of touch is being increasingly fine-tuned to the point of simulating the sensation of stirring thick substances. However, a crucial aspect of immersion is that the virtual traveller, as in the real world, can see and communicate with others who, similarly garbed, occupy and share the same virtual kingdom.

An unlikely candidate for one of the initial adventures into virtual reality is the creation of a rather undistinguished house by Division for Matsushita Electronic Industries (fig. 137). With its flock wallpaper and mediocre furniture and fittings, interior architectural excellence was not the goal. Instead, as manufacturers of heating and air-conditioning equipment as well as household electrical and electronic appliances, Matsushita commissioned this virtual world as a model for testing both the performance and the appearance of their products in a typical and fully operational two-storey Japanese house. Movement from one room to another is sensed in vision and sound via a headset; the physical interface being

Fig. 137: The interior of the Matsushita house created by Division.

sensed by a three directional mouse. The various positions and movements assumed by the hand-held mouse are ghosted in virtual reality by the image of a surrogate and disembodied grey hand which can perform a range of functions. In replicating the physical position of the mouse, the virtual hand can open and close doors, curtains and cabinet drawers; it can operate the lights and turn on taps - the latter action being accompanied by the realistic sound of running water. Other features in the house allow the Matsushita engineers and designers to study airflow patterns. For example, in the kitchen, steam, in the form of minute yellow and green droplets, rises from a boiling pot on the cooker, to enable the efficiency of the ceiling-mounted fume extractor to be analysed (see pages 144 & 145).

Although unconcerned with architectural statements, the Matsushita model does bring us some way towards the idea of the architect working in cyberspace. It also demonstrates the technological state of the art using leading edge systems and equipment, in this instance Divisions dVS software running on a Silicon Graphics Onyx platform.

Albeit confined to a screen, the ability of high-end CAD programmes to provide walkthroughs and flythroughs allows our mind's eye to take predetermined journeys through and around the dimensions of a design in flux. This ability is the important distinction that separates CAD from all former, traditional modes of 2D representation. What was a single, static and fixed viewpoint in space has become animated - a serial visual experience in which the spatial features of a design concept can, on demand, be viewed as a continuum from all possible and impossible vantage points.

In non-immersive and immersive constructs of virtual space it is apparent that the primary cue of motion parallax together with all secondary cues to depth are imported and present. However, by replicating all the faculties of human perception in a complete

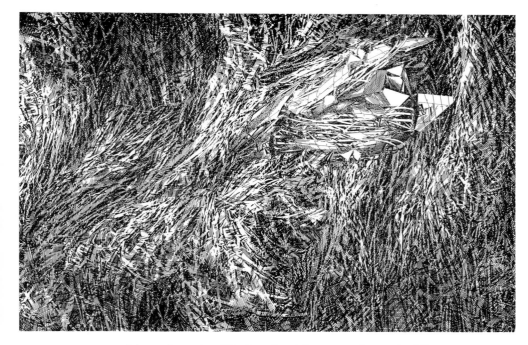

Fig. 138: Lebbeus Woods:
Turbulence Structure, 1991

and three-dimensional illusion of real time space, immersive VR systems place the act of designing in a radically new context. It is one in which the drawing board or the monitor screen is replaced by the ability directly to confront and fashion an architecture at full scale and complete with all its spatial variables. Furthermore, within this context the architect together with the client can wander around a design proposal in a new kind of partnership. If VR brings an unexpected setting in which architect and client can co-exist, it also brings the notion of a new rapprochement between them, plus the direct involvement of the client, and with this, the promise of a greater diversity in the outcome.

Architectural design, however, has not always been merely a process of creating actual buildings but also functions as a vehicle for pure architectural research, that is, a process of envisioning new concepts and ideas. Unfettered by the demands of clients and free from the limits of building technology, this ability to dream up a visionary architecture overtakes our ability to construct it. The paper dreams of an unbuilt environment exert a potent influence on mainstream thinking, its influence historically being traceable from the delineated dreamscapes of Piranesi to the gravity-defying habitats of Lebbeus Woods (fig. 138). According to Marcus Novak, the schism between such an architecture of the imagination and one rooted by its services and grounded by the laws of physics is converging rapidly. Our passage through the virtual door into cyberspace will allow Piranesi's monumental landscapes to be assembled and experienced; in cyberspace the levitating forms of Woods' Aerial Paris will actually fly. Not only will we experience them to full size and in context, we will also inhabit them. Moreover, it will not only be architects that occupy them, but everyone. They would function as virtual laboratories open to all.

Other issues are raised by the advent of this technology. For instance, the creation of an artificial world of inner space brings closer the idea of our escape into it. The concept of living and working in virtual space is already feasible. However, in order to accomplish this escape we would have to superimpose one reality on the other; to allow complete freedom of bodily locomotion along the interface we would have to overlay the virtual world upon a topological recognition of the physical world.

As to the future, there are two conflicting projections of an architecture of tomorrow. One sees virtual reality as inherently limited, incapable of providing actual shelter from the elements or replacing bodily functions and needs. Consequently, this vision argues, there will always be a need for a multiplicity of physical architecture, with VR supplying a cost-effective design dimension only. Another version sees real architecture becoming redundant, existing simply in the form of shed-like envelopes - virtual stations housing massive computer systems. In other words, the latter projection, in taking to extremes the notion of telepresence - virtual shopping, virtual banking, even virtual sex - envisions the architecture of the 21st century as an architecture of instruments, peopled by intelligent robotic agents extending and empowering our consciousness. Whichever is true, one thing is certain. The cybernetic augmentation of our physical experience will still require designers. This is because the spatial characteristics of cyberspace do not design themselves. So why not architects (or, as Nicholas Negroponte has recently suggested, who else but architects)? The architect could design both real and virtual environments or, at the very least, allow an exposure to cyberspace to reveal new ways of advancing and enhancing our understanding of a physical architecture.

In the past every architectural design began its life on a blank sheet of paper. It is well known that Joseph Paxton initially visualized his ideas for the Crystal Palace with a prophetic diagram scribbled on a blotting pad; that Oscar Niemeyer drafted the basic geometry of the form of Brazilia on the back of a cigarette packet, and that Charles Moore would doodle designs on a table napkin. The advent of a cybernetic technology, however, reverses the journey of a concept and turns the act of design outside-in. Instead of externalising ideas to experience them, the designer is dematerialized and transposed to be digitally represented by and within the same information system that represents the design. To coexist in the same space as occupied by our ideas, to become as one with a design, will bring new possibilities, new strategies and disclose previously invisible relationships. It also comes to question the very nature of our perception and, indeed, our understanding of reality. Above all, however, in detaching us from established aesthetic traditions, the new technology will finally release us from the confines of the drawing-board to confront a future environment full of the promise of unlimited richness and diversity.

Bibliography

Batterton, F., & Whiting, K., 'The Representation of Spatial Concepts in Architectural Design', Oxford Polytechnic, Oxford, 1974

Benedikt, M. (ed.), *Cyberspace, First Steps*, MIT Press, Boston, 1995

Broadbent, G., *Design in Architecture*, John Wiley & Sons, London, 1973

Coulton, J.J., *Greek Architects at Work*, Paul Elek, London, 1977

Davies, R., 'Montage', School of Architecture, Oxford Brookes University, Oxford, 1995

Gibson, J.J., *The Perception of the Visual World*, Allen & Unwin, London, 1950

Hall, E.T., *The Hidden Dimension*, Doubleday, New York, 1966

Harvey, J., *The Mediaeval Architect*, Wayward Publishers, London, 1972

Holl, S., *Anchoring*, Princeton University Press, New York, 1989

Lawson, B., *Design in Mind*, Butterworth Architecture, Oxford, 1994

Le Corbusier, *For Students Only: If I Had to Teach Students*, Faber, London, 1954

Lewin, K., *A Dynamic Theory of Personality*, McGraw Hill, New York, 1935

Levy, G.R., 'The Greek Discovery of Perspective: Its Influence on Renaissance and Modern Art', *Journal of the Royal Institute of British Architects*, January, 1943

Leyda, J., & Voynow, Z., *Eisenstein at Work*, Pantheon Books/The Museum of Modern Art, New York, 1982

Mitchell, W.J., *The Reconfigured Eye*, MIT Press, Boston, 1992

Morgan, C.L. & Zampi, G., *Virtual Architecture*, Batsford, London, 1995 (McGraw Hill, New York, 1995)

Mumford, L., 'Agents of Mechanization and the Eotechnic Phase', *Environments: Notes and Selections on Objects, Spaces and Behaviour*, Brooks/Cole, California, 1974

McCurdy, E., (trans.) *Leonardo da Vinci's Notebooks*, Duckworth & Co., London, 1907

Murphie, A., *The Wizard of Id*, School of Architecture, Oxford Brookes University, Oxford, 1996

Papanek, V., *Design for the Real World*, Thames & Hudson, London, 1972 (Bantam, New York, 1976)

Pikionis, A., *The Landscaping of the Archaeological Site around the Acropolis 1954-1957*, Bastas-Plessas Publications, Athens, 1994

Porter, T., *Architectural Drawing Master Class*, Studio Vista, London, 1993 (Van Nostrand Reinhold, New York, 1993)

Rheingold, H., *Virtual Reality*, Secker, 1991

Sommer, R., *Personal Space: The Behavioural Basis of Design*, Prentice Hall, New Jersey, 1943

Summerson, R., *How Needs Architecture?* Third Year Dissertation, School of Architecure, Oxford Brookes University, Oxford, 1995

Van de Ven, C., 'The Theory of Space in Architecture', *Companion to Contemporary Architectural Thought*, Routledge, London, 1993

Zevi, B., Architecture as Space, Horizon Press, New York, 1957

Index

Numbers in *italics* refer to illustration pages